BEGINNER'S GUIDE TO THAILAND

TOP BUCKET LISTS THAILAND TOUR WITH ME

A trip in Thailand by yourself in a way that you can choose the most important attractions in the central, northern, eastern and western regions, included 29 islands

By
Supennee K.B.
Tourist Guide License No. 11-76006

To my parents,

for always loving and supporting me.
I can't express how much my parents mean to me
and it seems that I have lost my best friends
when they passed away. I only can focus my
mind to wish them luck and happiness
for whatever they reborn,
that's all the best thing I can do.

Love you with all my heart.

The content and recommendations presented are not intended to be a substitute for a reader's tour program. The authors, photographs or participants in this book disclaim any liabilities or loss in the content of places and advice herein.

TABLE OF CONTENT

THE BOOK CONTENTS

➢ The 23 reasons, why you should go to Thailand. This topic can help you to decide and manage the trip before arrival.

➢ The summary of Thailand's historical background which aims for your brief information only.

➢ The names of 77 provinces in Thailand separated in each region for your information.

➢ The Central, Eastern, Western and the Northern Regions provinces included with their details of the remarkable places and how to go. For the north, I focused on Chiang Mai and Chiangrai, the main attractions of this region, where you should visit before other provinces in the north.

➢ The 29 islands in Thailand with their briefly backgrounds to explore.

ACKNOWLEDGEMENT

❑ I am eternally grateful to my parents who gave me life and love. Thank you for supporting me to study abroad to gain skills in English language.

❑ I am eternally grateful to all my guests I took care while I was a tour guide and to all I met during working at the tour counter. You made me a tour guide for years and all experiences I got are the great worth for the book and my works. I'm sorry if I did something that you might offend.

❑ I am more grateful to Dr. Glen; one of my guests who gave me The Family Word Finder Dictionary and many thanks for your support and kindness.

❑ I sincerely appreciate the kind support to all my customers who purchase the book. You have my deepest thanks. I really appreciate if you send me feedback or share some ideas to help me improve writing skill. We have met the bad time during Covid-19 together all over the world, but I believe that it's gone someday (I hope so soon). I wish I could see tourists' smiles again in Thailand.

❑ I am so very thankful for all information and photos shared from all app and media which allowed me to use for illustrations.

"Thanks very much to everyone on my publishing team."

Supennee K. B.

How to use the "Top Bucket Lists Thailand, Tour with me, and Beginner's Guide to Thailand:

- ❑ Please check how much time you have?
- ❑ If you have less than 7 hours in Thailand, please do not go out of the airport. You can enjoy the coffee shops, Thai restaurants or traditional Thai massage; most of them are on the 3rd or B Floor at the airport.
- ❑ If you have places in your mind, please see their details if it's fit for your time. Traffic in Bangkok is unpredictable for some places and sky trains takes time also. Be sure you won't miss your flight.
- ❑ Please check if my recommended tour options are suitable for the time you have. Each tour I recommended has its worth for your Thailand sightseeing.
- ❑ When you pick a choice or the recommended tour options, please go to the content pages to find out the details of the places. I made summary of the places for you to understand easily and helped you to decide what you should visit.

How to make travel worth the time you have in Thailand.

Transit Passengers from 7 hours or more:

You should have 2 hours for checking in and documents procedure; it means you have 5 hours left, I recommend you to visit a place nearby the Suwannaphum airport like, within **Samut Prakan** areas or travel by sky train to Phayathai and connect sky train to **Siam** for shopping and enjoy the downtown (It takes about 2 hours for traveling back and forth), you have three hours for walking around the malls; or get a car hire at the tour counter for a temple and city tour in Bangkok such as; The marble temple or Wat Pho for fast visiting and photo taking and enjoy the surroundings of those areas.

If it's Sunday, the traffic is not so jammed, you should go to The Grand Palace, the landmark of Thailand and admire the view of The Chao Phraya River. You can see more places within this area and nearby places.

***The temples are mainly opened early in the morning and closed about between 17.00-18.00 pm and the Grand Palace time is at 8.30 -15.30. The palace and / or Wat Phra Kaew may be closed during the royal ceremony. Please also check if the palace is opened for public the day you want to visit.

The other choice during Saturday-Sunday is by going to Jatujak Market. Get the airport link to Phayathai and connect the sky train to Mo Chit. Please always aware of the time you have, it's a large market with thousands shops where you can forget the departure time.

There are also some hotels for a temporary stay, if you're tired from the long flight (normally charged for 6 hours included with transport for pick-up and drop), you can check at the tour counter for the hotel rates before booking online.

Figure 1 Wat Phra Kaew

One full day in Thailand: (Each tour option recommended here is appropriated for one day in Bangkok)

- Must see; The Grand Palace and Wat Pho.
- One whole day for Ayutthaya Cruise Tour. (the tour started about 7.00 am- 18.00 pm)

Figure 2 the Grand Palace

- The riverboat trip for The Grand Palace, Wat Pho, Wat Arun and Wat Rakang and walk around both sides of the riverbanks.

- One day tour to Damnoensaduak Floating Market (Starting time is between 6.30-7.00 am) and visit Nakhon Pathom or back to visit some temples in Bangkok in the afternoon.

- The temples (Wat Trimit, Wat Pho and the Marble Temple) and look around the city.

- Ride the boat and visit the temples and the places nearby the river bank,

- Ancient City and Crocodile Farm.

- In case you would like to visit the beach, please go to Pattaya City early in the morning and visit The Sanctuary of Truth and a temple there, you can choose to stay overnight at Pattaya City instead of Bangkok because it's quiet near Suwannaphum Airport; taking about 2 hours ride there from the airport.

- Kanchanaburi for the bridge over the River Kwai and look around the town.

- Hua Hin; started early in the morning or stay overnight there and explore attractions next day but you need 3-4 hours riding to the airport. Please always make sure you have already checked in. Don't take luggages; except the necessary personal things, with you when you want to tour. The Left-Luggages Room is available at the second floor of the Suwannaphum Airport.

- Suphanburi province is also close to Bangkok where you can admire some old temples and a large aquarium at Bueng Chavak, you should see its detail.

- One day and one night is also good to go to Khao Yai for relaxing in the nature surroundings and admire some temples there. (Don't go in rainy season; Jun-Sep)

- Lopburi is also a good destination for one day trip.

3-4 days in Thailand:

- Two days for exploring Bangkok Metropolitan Region (Bangkok, Nonthaburi, Pathumthani, Nakhon Pathom, Samut Prakan and Samut Sakon) plus one night at Pattaya beach or Kanchanaburi or Ayuttaya.
- The Grand Palace and temples in Bangkok; Wat Trimit, Wat Pho, The Marble Temple, Wat Saketh, Wat Ratchanadda, Wat Intraviharn, Wat Suthat, etc. plus one-two nights in Pattaya City.
- Phuket Island and one day in Bangkok for The Grand Palace and places nearby.
- Samui Island and one day in Bangkok for The Grand Palace and places nearby.
- Enjoy Bangkok, Damnoen Saduak, Ayutthaya and Kanchanaburi.
- Chiang Mai or Chiangrai and one night in Bangkok for a half day tour to The Grand Palace.

Figure 3 Wat Tang sai, Prachup Khiri khun

5-7 days or more in Thailand

Must see: The Grand Palace, the temples, local market, ride sky train all over Bangkok, Damnoensaduak Floating market, Ayutthaya and Kanchanaburi plus;

➤ Hua Hin, Pattaya City, Koh Chang, Sattaheep
➤ Explore islands, like Phuket, Samui, Pha-gnan, Phan-gna and other islands nearby. (For Andaman Sea; Oct-Dec, and Jan-Apr for the Gulf of Thailand)
➤ Enjoy the north at Chiang Mai / Chiangrai and one night in Bangkok.
➤ Explore the rural areas and the cultural world heritage by UNESCO at Sukhothai and Kam Phaeng Phet before going to Chiang Mai.

Why Thailand is very popular?

The 23 reasons for visiting Thailand will give you the ideas for your plan, **how** you will arrange your trip, **where** you should go, **when** you should come here, **what** your vacation will be and **whom** you will be with!

1. **Thailand is the Land of Smile and Warm Hospitality. Part of our culture is giving a "Wai" to each other; for greeting, welcome, introduction and thanking.**

Giving a "Wai" in general; is by connecting your palms together between your chests and lower your head until the nose touches the index fingers. There are some forms of "Wai" like, paying respect to others especially the elderly people who sit; we sit on the floor in a position of squatting and wai.

Wai for Buddha Statue or monk is by kneeling on the floor or sit on the legs and wai. But during religious rituals, we "Krab"; by pressing the thumbs between the eyebrows and bend down the head (it's like a child-pose in yoga) with the palms on the floor three times.

Krab three times is for paying homage to Buddha, Dhamma (Buddha's Teaching) and Sankha (His disciples or ordained monk). Krab is normally done when we pay homage to the statues of Buddha in ordination hall, Viharn hall and pagoda in the temple.

Wai comes with saying **"Sawasdee Ka"** while men saying **"Sawasdee Krub"** for hello, good morning etc.

Ka and Krub are suffix added during speaking for showing politeness.

"**Kob Khun**" means "Thank You"

We smile to each other even we don't know each other before and giving a Wai to others for thanking or asking for help. Smiling always comes along with Wai every time.

The favorite words you may hear from Thai:
"**Sawasdee**" means good morning, afternoon, evening, hello, hi, and goodbye.

"**Kin Kow Rue Yang?**" means "Did you have breakfast? Or Lunch? Or "Dinner". **Kin** means Eat, **Kow** means Rice, **Rue Yang** means Did you? We usually call Kow for the meals; but if you would like to mention "Breakfast", you can say "Kow Chow", "Lunch" is "Kow Klang Wan" and "Dinner" is "Kow Yen".

Chow is morning, Klang wan is noon time and Yen is evening.

"**Pai Nai**" means "Where are you going?"

"**Kor Toad**" means; when you do mistakes; like, saying sorry, excuse, apologize to someone, but can also say during someone's speaking or have a conversation, or asking for help from others you don't know.

"**Mai Pen Rai**" means "Never mind", "It's O.K"

"**Mai Mee Pan-ha**" means "No problem",   "No worry"

Don't forget to add "Ka" and "Krub" for woman and man and smile!

Please notice that, the English spelling for Thai words are spelled according to their pronunciation, so they maybe written different. For example; the word "Ayutthaya", may be written "Ayuddhaya", or "Nakhon Pathom" maybe written "Nakonpathom" etc.

Friendship is easily found in Thailand.

2. Thailand is Low Budget for your entire traveling.

The food and accommodation are cheap and good. You can find food by the street or even in some restaurants; like, 50 Bahts a meal.

• International fast food, grocery stores, superstores and 7/11 are found everywhere for your fast meal and some personal items.

The accommodations are very cheap such as; hotels (started from 500 Bahts), guesthouses (started from 150 Bahts), homestays, condo, apartments, hostels, houses for rent and resorts.

• If you prefer elegant and luxury hotels, they are also available everywhere in Thailand. The grade of hotels depends on the locations you choose.
• The good locations which are convenient and comfortable such as; Silom Rd., Sukhumvit Soi 1-101, Khaosan Road, Siam Square, Yaowaraj, Riverside areas, Nearby airports, Nearby Democracy monument, Nearby Victory monument, Nearby sky train stations, Soi Aree, Saphan Kwai areas and Ratchada Road.

Nowadays, the transports are convenient. Almost everywhere in Bangkok have sky trains and subways so tourists can choose many nice hotels with low prices along the suburb.

You can find also accommodations in every province which are nice and lower prices. Try to stay in downtown of each district for your safety. Travelling in low season (May-Sept) will save your money indeed. **The transports** are also cheap; such as, public buses, vans, Tuk Tuk; sky trains (BTS), subways (MRT), taxi, motorcycle-taxi, car rent and even tours.

3. Thailand has both mirrors of modernization and the rural locations.

You can still see the old style of living in the upcountry or nearby Bangkok. You still also see some wooden houses along the riverbank in Bangkok or other market places somewhere and see people wear local clothes; like, robes wrapped around and some merchants with old style of carrying poles for selling stuffs walking in the big cities where mainly dense with tall buildings like in Bangkok, Chiang Mai, Phuket, Khon Khean, Nakorn Ratchasima, Hat Yai and Pattaya City.

Figure 4 Farmers and carts are seen everywhere in upcountry.

4. Thailand is easy and convenient for travelling around the country by variety of

good system and modern Transports.

From **Suwannaphum International airport;** you can start your trip by your own easily. We have **taxi meters and public-buses** on the 1st Floor, **car hire** on 2nd Floor, **BTS** or Airport Link at the Basement Floor (you can connect MRT or subways by this Airport Link skytrain) to downtown.

If you prefer more comfortable and save time for travelling to your hotel and don't mind the prices, then choose **Tour Services and AOT on 2nd Floor** for going to your hotel; by showing your destination and checking the prices at their counters, this is the best way for taking you to the right place you book, especially; when you are first time in Thailand.

Domestic flights are affordable prices and convenient to all regions. There are 2 airports; Suwannaphum and Don Muang in Bangkok.

Tuk-Tuk or "Sam-raw" are good for short trip only. Always ask the price before riding and don't let him wait for you. They are not tourist guide so please consider when they offer you too cheap for a tour.

Sky trains and **subways** are more comfortable and convenient for seeing all over Bangkok.

Taxi Meter; please choose the new car and photo the registered no. inside the car, make sure you have address of your destination to show to them.

Ferry Boats, River Boats, shuttle boats and Express Boats are available for avoiding traffic on the road, but don't ride the crowded boats.

Local trains to other provinces are available at the main railway station; it's at Bang Sue Grand Station near Chatuchak Park. You can book a train at Hua Lum Phong Station also.

*Some of the tours need a tourist guide; it's not only to save your time but you can relax and feel more comfortable.

5. Thai Food is delicious and spicy.

The Thai food has a variety of flavors and quiet unique recipes. The mixture of all ingredients makes the taste mellow and perfect in all dishes.

It makes you have a good appetite anytime you see or just smell it. Whenever you taste a Thai meal; whether in a restaurant or from vendors by street, you will definitely feel good and enjoy all of them.

Figure 5 Fried egg with rice and sweet and sour shrimps

The food cost you with reasonable prices and you can find something to eat 24 hours in Thailand.

I would like to recommend the famous typical Thai food you should try:

THAI FOOD

Figure 6 Tom Yum Koong

Tom-yum Koong (Shrimp spicy Soup with mixed herbal plants, fresh chili, and lime juice and fish sauce) it's good when it's served suddenly after cooking and it's perfect with steam rice.

Pad Thai (Fried Rice Noodle and shrimps or prawns mixed with special sauce which taste sweet and sour; (the sauce made from tamarind juice and brown sugar) served with bean sprouts and chives.

Figure 7 Pad Thai

Pad Kra-prow; a hot and spicy fried meat and herbal basil leaves), this is a Thai popular dish; we order this on top of rice and a fried egg which is enough for one meal. It costs about 50 Bahts from street or a small restaurant or food court.

Curry; a kind of spicy soup from coconut milk mixed with green or red chili paste added some vegetables and meat. It's super delicious from chilli paste made of great finesse by the cook.

Massaman Curry; its taste is known sweet curry from the mixed spicy chili paste and peanuts for curry sauce. It's cooked with meat, potatoes, onions and tomatoes. This dish is similar to Indian food but more tasty and spicy to be typical Thai style dish. It's mostly popular among tourists.

Panang Curry; is different from Pad Panang, it's more mild chili paste mixed with coconut milk cooked with meat and basil leaves.
Pad Panang; (Red Chili paste stir fried with meat and sometimes mixed with vegetables)

Larb is the local northeastern and northern dishes. It's the mixture of ground meat and herbal plants include chilli powder for spicy taste; the difference between the two regions, are the tastes and some ingredients. Larb becomes the signature dishes for anyone who goes to the provinces within those regions. It's nice to eat spicy somtum and Larb with sticky rice. Must try!

Main ingredients; onion, garlic, chili, etc.

Som Tum

Yum

❖ **Som-Tum or Papaya salad;** hot and spicy pepper with fresh garlic pounded with raw and crispy chopped papaya, dry tiny shrimps, peanuts, lime juice and tomatoes added. It's good to eat with fried or grilled chicken and sticky rice.

- **Yum** is kinds of Thai salad but the mixtures are hot peppers, vegetable and grilled meat. (Spicy taste is recommended.)
- Fried or Steamed fish/meat/seafood with spicy chili sauce or sweet and sour sauce. It's a seafood dish where you can find in any restaurants.
- Rice / Egg Noodles or Plain Rice soup; a bowl of noodle is called "Kua Tiew" and a bowl of rice is called "Kow Thom"; it's mixed with meat balls or sliced/ground meats in soup and spring onion. It is the light meal and helps you getting rid of hungry very well. Find them everywhere and mostly are Street food.
- **Fried Rice** with /without meat is popular for fast meal or "made to order" cooked by the vendors nearby streets and restaurants.

- **Stir Fried meat or without meat;** is "made to order" cooked by vendors, for people who are selective for the meal; for example, some are Vegan, some don't eat beef, some don't eat some kinds of vegetables etc.
- **Moo Krata/ Suki/;** the hot pot for grilling or cooking by you in a restaurant; served with raw meat, vegetables and unique sauces. It's popular among the family and a group of friends, by sitting around the stove and enjoys cooking together.
- **Khow Kaeng** is a meal for easy, fast and save money for rush hour during working days; there are many small restaurants or vendors with their trolleys full of their ready-made food and rice to help rushed people for fast meal.   **ETC.**

❖ **Food at Food court** in malls or department stores are good to try. You can find variety of street food to try at Food Court of Suwannaphum Airport on 1st Floor.

❖ **International Food** found in many places; like, restaurants, hotels or some department stores with food courts, community malls, or neighborhoods of tourist areas.

❖ **Buffet** at some hotels; many hotels provide Buffet Breakfast, Lunch and Dinner with variety of International food with affordable prices. It's a choice for having meals at a nice and cozy place.

❖ **Superstores, local market and grocery stores;** provide raw food and things you need for daily uses, are found almost everywhere. There are nice food packed for ready-to-eat and it's OK.

❖ **7/11 or other convenient stores** are everywhere for serving you all the time.

Khanom Tuay

Khanom SaiSai

Khanom Thong Yib/Thong Yod

Khanom Chan

how Niew Mamuang

Khanom Piek Poon

Khanom Thabtim Krop

Figure 8 Khanom or Thai Dessert

FRUITS IN THAILAND

Figure 9 Dragon fruit, rose apple, mango and jackfruit

❖ There are many typical **Thai fruits** known all over the world like; Mango (Please try ripe mango with sticky rice), Durian, Rambutan, Longan, Pineapple, Orange, Banana, Lychee, Papaya, Dragon fruit, Grape, Mangosteen, Water melon, Guava, Tammarind, Jackfruit, Pomegranate, Strawberry, Avocado, Custard Apple etc.

❖ You can find many nice fruits in superstores and in a local market. Try to eat the fruits in season.

Fruits in Nov-Jan; grape, ripe papaya, rose apple, guava, pine apple, sugar cane, jujube, water melon, sapodilla,

Fruits in Feb-May; tamarind, grape, water melon, banana, jackfruit, mango, durian, lychee, rambutan,

Fruits in Jun-Oct; mangosteen, ripe papaya, bananas, Thai melon, longan, pomelo, orange, guava, custard apple

Please go to Talat Or Tor Kor nearby Jatujak Market where there are plenty of fruits and delicious meal. (It's not so far from the airports, BTS: at Mo Chit Station and walk about 10 mins. MRT: at Kham Phaeng Petch Station is direct to the market.

6. Thailand is full of festivals all year round in all over the country.

You can check the events when you reach the hotel or if you suppose to visit Thailand for big events, please check the events from the hotel you book. The big events are usually planned and announced in every province.

Most of festivals are performed inside the temples but some of them are with parades in the center of town and some are performed at some public areas like, market, malls, city pillar shrine, etc.

Several of festivals are related to Buddhism and traditions of the old town sites and dated according to the Full Moon Day of Buddhist Lunar Calendar. Kathin Tradition is one of the most popular for Thai Buddhist; the tradition is to offer the monk robe to a temple where lack of robes and to create harmony among the people who comes from different places to join this ritual after the Lent Day. It's only a month period for this festival and it's important for Thai Buddhists and temples in nationwide.

Figure 10 Kathin Tradition; during Kathin Robe Parade.

THAI FESTIVALS

The famous festivals in nationwide are Songkran Day Festival; the grand festival of Thailand with the public holidays are in between 13th-15th April, is known as Thai New Year Celebration which may last up to 10 days. The other is Loy Krathong Day Festival; on Full Moon Day in November during high tide.

Figure 11 Pouring water on Buddha Statue and to the elderly on Songkran Day

SONGKRAN FESTIVAL

This is "The Water Festival" of the country. The people use water and a nice fragrant powder to greet each other on New Year Celebration. The meaning of water festival is "Fresh and clean"; for welcoming good things to life, wash away the sufferings, anxiety and distress.

The tradition has been held since the ancient time with the beliefs that if we pay respects by pouring the water upon the Buddha Statues and the statues of the important Monks, bath the parents; or the elderly in family, the monks in the temples nearby homes; we will be blessed for being lucky and happy. We sometimes only pour on their hands but bathing parents have been a long-standing tradion in Songkran Day.

Sand Pagoda is an old tradition during Songkran Day; found only in Thailand and Laos nowadays; from the Buddhist's belief since ancient time; to pay respect to Buddha and to express apology for taking the soil on the feet (by walking in temple's area) from the temple.

Figure 12 Tradition of Pouring the water to the monks

Figure 13 Sand Pagoda made on Songkran Festival

The fun time of Water-Festival among the young and children are by by shooting or splashing water in the streets from plastic guns. Khaosan Road and Silom Road is the most popular places in Bangkok. Chiang Mai is a place where most Tourists think of this festival.

April is the beginning of the hot season in Thailand and people enjoy this Water Festival very much. Parties are everywhere during this long vacation in the hottest time of the year.

Each region has its own culture of Songkran Day Festival; but with the same belief among Thai, it's the Family Day, the day people await Songkran Day to have a chance to be back to hometowns to meet parents and all members in their family. Not only to enjoy each other but also can do merits by offerings and set free animals during the long holiday together at least once a year.

There are several incidents during Songkran Day Festival you should be careful: Traffic jams are along the roads to all regions and cause many accidents. Many hotels in the tourist areas are fully booked. Many famous restaurants are crowded with customers. Mostly tickets for all kinds of transportation are fully booked and drunkards are around the town because everyone stops working and enjoy the parties.

Loy Kra-Thong Day Festival is famous for fireworks and riverboat parties during the high tide on Full Moon Day in November; after Buddhist Lent Day one month.

"Kra-thong" is blooming lotus shaped baskets made from banana leaves decorated with flowers and lighted candles with incent sticks for paying respect to The Goddess of the Rivers. It's the belief that if we ask for forgiveness from the Goddess of Rivers, to forgive us the bad things we have done like, throwing things to the rivers and canals anywhere before, we will get a good wish come to life.

The glittering of plenty Krathongs floating along the waterways give a picturesque view and amazing night by the river all over the country.

The grand Loy Krathong Festival is well known as **YI PENG OR THE LANTERN FESTIVAL;** a famous tradition and well known in **Chiang Mai at Ping River**. Several lanterns are released to the sky, it's nice to see but you have to be careful the fire.

The Candle Festival is one of the famous festivals at Ubon Ratchathani Province in the northeast region; or called as "Isan" by locals. It's one of the tourist attractions for Thai and foreigners. The tradition of Candle Parades happens during The Buddhist Lent Day every year; it's a day after Full Moon Day on the 8th Month of the Buddhist Lunar Calendar.

Many big candles are carved into different images related to Buddhism with the decorations and performed by the people or the groups of communities and agencies of the province. It's fantastic to see all beautiful carved candle parades in the street for The Candle Parade Contest at the center of Ubon Ratcha Thani Town.

Figure 14 Maekhong River and Nongkai Province

The other one of the famous festivals in Isan Region is called **"Bunk Fai Phaya Nak"** Festival on the day when The Buddhist Lent Day ends. People go to Nong Kai Province for watching this strange phenomenon. They are natural phenomena of lights overspread from Mae Khong River to the sky and it's believed by worshippers that; the lights come from Phaya Nak; a mystical serpent in the river during paying homage to Buddha's Relic.

Figure 15 Festivals; Bunk Fai, Candle Festival, Phi Ta Khon, Chinese New Year

MORE OF INTERESTING   FESTIVALS

o **THE VEGETARIAN FESTIVAL IN PHUKET.**
o **PHI TA KHON (GHOST FESTIVAL) IN LOIE.**
o **MONKEY BUFFET IN LOPBURI.**
o **UMBRELLA FESTIVAL IN CHIANG MAI.**
o **ELEPHANT FESTIVAL IN SURIN.**
o **CHINESE NEW YEAR FESTIVAL IN BANGKOK.**

There are many more of traditions in Thailand. Most of them are related to the remarkable places of each province such as; the important pagodas, Buddha Images, an old community of town and other religious rituals. Please check from the hotels or people in areas wherever you are.

7. Thailand is Safe for Travelling.

If you choose the hotel-address of the downtown areas where surrounded by many residences you'll feel as if you are living at one of your home. Avoid all the places people rarely stay or go to like; it's too cheap or very far from the center. Please get a place nearby sky trains or popular areas in downtown of Bangkok. Try to use public transports like; trains, buses, river boats, ferry boats, Song Thaew (a public pick-up truck with 2 row seats) or by walking. Join a tour service for first time visiting Bangkok; it's the best way to know the city very well from the licensed tourist guide and I think it's the best way to help you to learn about locals.

Most of Thai characteristics are friendly and helpful people and this is one of the charms for Thailand where you want to visit more than once.

8. Thailand is full of National Parks and Adventurous places that keep you excited in many homes of wildlife all the year.

You may accidentally see some wild elephants along the roads you pass somewhere!

There are varieties of jungle activities; like, trekking, hiking, nature trails, camping, fresh water rapids rafting, zip line, jumping, camping in many national parks in every province. You should get details from the National Parks Office from their websites for accommodations, checking the weather and activities they allow tourists that time.

9. Thailand is full of Beaches and Sunshine.
Thailand's territorial waters have more than 900 islands distributed in 19 provinces; the biggest island is Phuket, then Samui, Chang, Talutau, Pha Ngan and Kood Islands respectively. The province which has the most islands is **Phan-gna** Province, with 155 islands, then **Krabi** Province, with 154 islands and **Suratthani** Province, with 108 islands.

About 521 beaches distributed in 21 provinces; by 360 beaches of the Gulf of Thailand and 161 beaches of Andaman Sea.

Many couples choose Thailand for honeymoon and spend long vacation in many islands. Staying at town resorts and hotels which full of facilities and entertainments make the trip fun and full of joys.

There are 29 islands in this book contents for you to explore. Many of water activities like; scubadiving, snorkeling, ski, surfing, swimming, nature trails to make your dream destination perfect.

10.Thailand is full of rich culture and many archaeological sites from the long history.

There are about 40,000 temples and monasteries in Thailand. All the temples are called "Wat"; most of the temples are full of ancient architectures and sculptures.

Not only temples you can visit but there are museums to tell about historical backgrounds for all provinces you go.

The museums can help you to get more details about Thailand's history rather than other information. The national museum in Bangkok is very interesting place you should visit. Its location is near The Grand Palace where you can only walk to the place which is near Thammasat University.

The reason why Thailand is full of temples is because most of the populations are mainly Buddhists. Temples are found anywhere you go. You should try to visit temples you meet because it may be the temple where the historical evidences of Thai culture, festivals, traditions, people, artifacts and many of ancient items are found.

Figure 16 Ban Chiang, Udonthani

Figure 17 Thailand and neighbors

11. Thailand is Convenient to Travel to other Southeastern Countries and other countries nearby.

Once you are in Thailand, you may add our neighbored countries in your lists so you can make your vacation more valuable in one time traveling to Southeast Asia.

✓ **Laos** is connected to the north and northeast of Thailand. You can go by public buses from north eastern Terminal in Bangkok, trains and by direct flights to Vientian or Luang Phrabang (for 1 hour). You can also drive the car there by crossing the borders. There are many boundary posts in many provinces such as Nan, Uttaradit, Phayao, Chiang Rai, Loei, Nong Kai, Nakhon Phanom, Bueng Kan, Mukda Harn, and Ubon Ratchathani.

✓ **Vietnam**, you can travel from Laos easily by bus or travel by planes from Thailand.

✓ **Cambodia**; there are boundary posts in Si Saketh, Surin, Sa Kaew, Chanthaburi and Trat Provinces. You can ride public buses or vans to reach the checkpoints.

✓ **Myanmar**; there are boundary posts in Chiang Rai, Chiang Mai, Mae Hong Sorn, Tak, Kanchanaburi, Prachub Khiri Khun, and Ranong Provinces. Travel by plane is more convenient.

✓ **Malaysia**; there are boundary posts in Yala, Satoon, Songkla and Narathiwas Provinces. You can go by bus, train and car to cross the border.

✓ **You can also catch the planes to Hong Kong, Singapore and Indonesia conveniently from Thailand.**

Figure 18 Thai-Laos Friendship Bridge

12. Thailand has a pleasant weather for your all year-round destination.

Although it's Monsoon Season, it's still a good time for visiting Thailand; especially, in the northern region like; Chiang Mai, Chiang Rai, Nan, Tak, and Mae Hong Sorn for admiring fascinating scenery of green forests and mountainous areas where there are homestays or resorts for your accommodations. **You will find it's cheaper than the hot season with pleasant climate!**

13. Thailand has many kinds of Markets.

Everywhere you go or walk by the streets, you see a market or vendors selling something like; fresh food, fruits, clothes, second hand products, used cars, electrical appliances, antiques, Buddha Statues and religious supplies, gold and jewelry, street food vendors, furniture.

Flea markets for food are found in all sub-districts and in downtown both day and night.

There are food vendors at night market or as locals call "Talat Tho Lung"; which means "Markets till morning". This kind of market is very fond among Thai people because some of them work late at night. The market is full of delicious food and some market has souvenirs for selling to tourists. It's not hot at night so the people feel relaxed and more comfortable than the day time. Hua Hin Town is famous for Talat tho Lung among tourists.

14. **Thailand has six cultural and natural World Heritage sites by UNESCO World Heritage Convention:**

THE CULTURAL AND NATURAL WORLD HERITAGE SITES BY UNESCO

❖ **Ayutthaya Historical Park; was declared a cultural world heritage site in 1991 of a true national Thai Art,** located at the center of Ayutthaya Province, 75 Kilometers from Bangkok. The sites include Wat Ratchaburana, Wat Mahathat, Wat Phra Srisanpetch, Wat Phra Ram and The Hall of Phra Monkol Borpit.

❖ **Sukhothai Historic Park was** declared a cultural world heritage site in 1991. The areas are part of the Historic Town of Sukhothai and Associated Historic Towns. The site also includes with the associated historical parks in Kham-Phaeng-Phet province and Sri Satchanalai District of Sukhothai. Sukhothai Historic Park is in Sukhothai Province; the northern region, nearby the center of town, away from Bangkok about 440 kilometers and the other is in Kampaeng Peth is nearby province to the south of Sukhothai. **Inside remains the royal palace and twenty-six temples.**

❖ **Thungyai-Huai Kha Khaeng Wildlife Sanctuary coupled with Thung Yai Naresuan Wildlife sanctuary was declared** a natural world heritage site in 1991. The total land is about 1,536,296.29 acres, homes of a large number of wild animals and plants; like all other sites in mainland of Southeast Asia. The two sanctuaries located at Uthaithani, Tak and Kanchanaburi Provinces.

Figure 19 Huai Kha Khaeng Wildlife Sanctuary

❖ **Ban Chiang Archaeological Site was declared a cultural world heritage site in 1992 according to its ancient and red pottery** which describe the site of unique cultural tradition of livings and civilization of about 5000 years ago. The site is in Udorn-thani Province; located at the northeastern region or called as "Isan" for Thai; the distance is about 650 kms from Bangkok. There are flights to go to Udonthani.

You can travel to Udonthani by public buses at the Northern Bus Terminal at Mo Chit; ride the skytrain from the airport to Mo Chit Station and catch a taxi there or get the train to this province from Bang Sue Grand Station.

Udonthani is one of the provinces, close to the Nongkai province; the border of Laos, where you can start exploring Isan Provinces from here easily. It's a large town with many attractions. Don't miss to admire the bautiful pagoda at Wat Pah Ban Thad; the famous temple since Luang Ta Phra Maha Bua was alive (1913-2011); he's the former abbot who's a leader of many of "Phra Pah" or "Forest Monks" to access to the Buddha's Teaching from his Concentration Learning for Mindfulness and become worshipped among not only; the monks but also the people in Thailand and others. He started for the help Thai Nation Project; a charitable effort dedicated to helping the Thai economy and brought tons of gold to the Treasury.

❖ **Dong Pha-yayen-Khao Yai Forest Complex** was declared the natural world heritage site in 2005; with the areas of Dong Phraya Yen and its group; namely, Khao yai, Thap Lan, Pang Sida, Ta Phraya National Parks and Dong Yai wildlife Sanctury. The total lands

are 6,155 Square Kilometers which cover the 6 provinces; Nakorn-ratchsima, Saraburi, Nakornnayok, Prachinburi, Sa Keaw and Buriram Provinces. It has been called as "The East Forest of Thailand". **Khao Yai; a famous and popular attraction among tourists,** is the first National Park of Thailand situated in Nakorn- ratchasima province where are homes of wild elephants; which seen along the road.

Figure 20 Khaeng Krachan National Park

❖ **Khaeng Krachan National Park;** the largest national park in Thailand was recently named a UNESCO World Heritage Site on July 26, 2021. It consists of rainforest on the eastern slope of The Tanasserim Mountain Range; the border line between Thailand and Myanmar, with the highest peak of 1,513 meters above medium sea level, with many wildlife and rare plants found here. The climate is very humid with heavy rains. The tourist attractions are opened only during August-October in the areas of Khao Phanoen Thung and Ban Krang.

Kaeng Krachan is one of the popular destinations of adventurers for camping and Butterfly lovers. One of amazing Thailand Tours is to see swarm of butterflies all over the land in April here.

15. Thailand has many amazing local products and handicrafts from each Local Village which are very unique and best souvenirs for all tourists.

. We are well known for OTOP or One Tambon-One Product; Tambon means sub-district, where the locals produce their home products to their communities.

You can find all products easily in the markets or department stores cost from 10 to millions Bahts. Many various products or goods are popular found cheap prices at Jatujak Market or Week-end market in Bangkok (at Mo Chit Sky train BTS station or Kham Phaeng Phet station by MRT)

**There is a big event at Impact Exhibition Center (the place is not so far from the airports) for OTOP products every year. The huge exhibition halls are where you can enjoy shopping from all regions in Thailand together with culture shows to create the atmosphere of each region. Normally it happens in November-February. Don't miss it! It's nice to walk around the air-con areas from 10 am-22.00pm.

Figure 21 Thai Silk

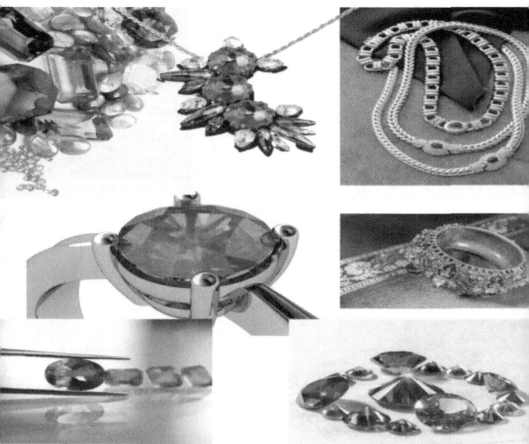

16. **Thailand is one of the top countries in the world exporting gems and jewelry products.**
    You can find some nice jewelry anywhere from the low prices (in silver-setting) until many millions.

    The collections of the precious stones with high quality are from reliable stores with product guaranteed. They are popular gifts for your beloved ones or yourselves. The famous gem stones are **Rubies and Sapphires in Thailand**. Chan-tha-buri Province is famous for precious stone mines, but the center market is in Bangkok.

    Thai Silk is also best known for elegant and unique designs and colors.

Figure 22 Novice ordination ceremony

17. Thailand has many Centers of Meditation Practices and is popular for Buddhist Monk Ordinations from foreigners.

About 95% of populations are Buddhists in Thailand and a tradition for Thai men when they reach 20 years old should be ordained as monks.

You need to ask permission for ordination in the temple you want to be ordained as a monk, however; being a monk, is not only shaving your hair and wearing the monk robes but strictly for being in discipline, by practicing meditation and chanting in Pali language. Concentrating in learning the Essence of Buddha's Teaching is the way to find Purity of Mind and be free from sufferings.

The popular occasion for ordination is before Buddhist Lent Day and the ordained monks normally stay in monkhood until the end day of Lent which takes about 3 months. Some of them are monks for life.

"Precepts" traditions for general Buddhists who want to observe are five precepts and eight precepts during the Buddha's Day for receiving merits. People stay in the temple for one night or sometimes for longer period as they want for practicing chanting, meditation and help the work in the temple. This traditional practice has been held since the ancient time. There are many foreigners; both men and women observe the 5 and 8 precepts in some temple.

Figure 23 Dinosau images

18. Thailand has many kinds of Entertainments and Amusement Parks for the family tourists in all major provinces of each region.

19. Thailand has a good Public Health System. We have lots of modern hospitals and medical clinics with high technology almost every province.

20. Thailand is very cosmopolitan and international. There are many global food, stores, product chains and imported goods from all over the world.

21. Thailand has an amazing Nightlife you must not miss. You can enjoy nightlife every province.
22. Thailand has known for the popular destination to Koh Phagnan for "The Full Moon Party". The island is where the most beautiful view of Full Moon shines in Surat Thani. You need to plan for the flights and the boat trip there.

23. Thailand is named "Venice of The East". There are several canals in Bangkok and other provinces. Many of floating markets are almost seen everywhere you are near the rivers or canals.

Figure 24 Ko Pha Gnan and Full Moon Party

The original Floating Market that sill keep old styles of living by canals is at Dam Noen Saduak District in Ratchaburi Province; where you can see vendors on a small boat or "Sampan" Boat, carry their fruits and food along the canals to the center of market. It's about 120 kilometers from Bangkok.

Some of the floating markets are made to simulate the atmosphere of the original one and also are popular among tourists.

Figure 25 Thailand map

BRIEFLY HISTORICAL BACKGROUND OF THAILAND

Area

Thailand or Siam or the Kingdom of Thailand is the country in the Southeast Asia. It composed of 77 provinces with the area of 513,120 square kilometers (198,120 sq. Mile) located at the center of the Indochinese Peninsula.

Our language is Thai language. The population is approximately 70 million.

BANGKOK is the capital of Thailand.

Neighbors

Thailand **borders** Myanmar in the north and the west, Laos in the north and the northeast, Cambodia in the east and southeast and the gulf of Thailand and Malaysia in the south. There is The Andaman Sea on the western side.

Weather

The weather in Thailand is tropical and hot; there are mainly two seasons in nationwide, the Monsoon season (June-October) and the dry season (November-May). The temperature is about 22-35 Celsius.

Winter in Thailand

The provinces for cold weather are Nan, Chiang Rai, Phayao, Mae Hong Sorn and Mountainous Areas or "Doi" everywhere in the northern region. The temperature is 0-10 Celsius. (November-February)

Religion

Buddhism is our main religion (95% of population). Others are Islam, Christianity, Hinduism and others.

Politics and Government

Thailand is a constitutional monarchy and parliamentary democracy. The present king is King Wachiralongkorn (King Rama 10th of Juckree Dynasty; the only son of King Bhumibol (King Rama 9th and Queen Sirikit.) The head of government and the leader of the cabinet is the prime minister.

Thai Currency

Our currency is called **Baht.** The banknotes are 1000, 500, 100, 50, and 20 Baht. The coin notes are 10, 5, 2, 1 Baht and small ones are 50 and 25 Satangs. (100 Satangs equal 1 Baht)

Thailand is classified as a newly industrialized economy; manufacturing, agriculture and tourism are leading sectors of the economy.

There are six geographical regions in Thailand; Central, North, East, West, South and Northeast regions.

Figure 26 Regional Thai Dance; left to right, Isan, South, North and Central at the middle

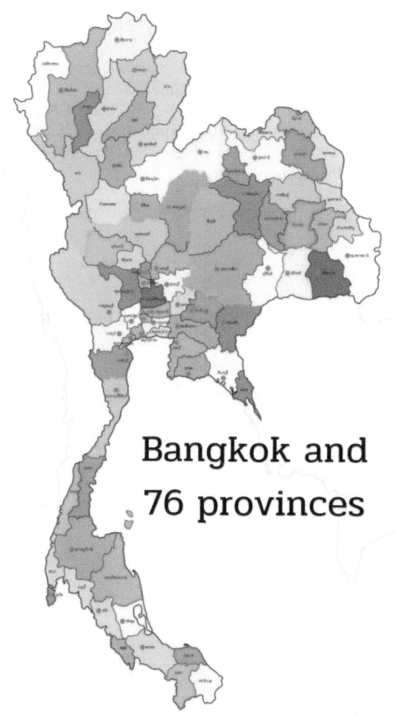

Bangkok and
76 provinces

Figure 27 Map of 77 provinces in Thailand

CENTRAL REGION:

Bangkok, Nonthaburi, Pathum Thani, Nakhon Pathom, Samut Prakan, Samut Sakhon, Samut Songkram, Phra Nakhon Si Ayutthaya, Ang Thong, Singburi, Chainat, Lopburi, Saraburi, Suphanburi, Nakhon Nayok, Nakhon Sawan, Uthai Thani, Sukhothai, Phitsanulok, Phichhit, Kam Phaeng Phet, Phetchabun.

WEST REGION:

Tak, Kanchanaburi, Ratchaburi, Phetchaburi and Prachub Khiri Khun.

EAST REGION:

Chachoengsao, Chanthaburi, Chonburi, Prachinburi, Rayong, Sa Kaew and Trat.

NORTH REGION:

Chiang Mai, Lamphun, Lampang, Chiang rai, Phayao,
Mae Hong Sorn, Nan, Phrae and Uttaradit.

SOUTH REGION:

Chumphon, Ranong, Nakhon Si Thammarat, Surat Thani, Trang, Phuket, Narathiwat, Pattani, Phatthalung, Songkhla, Yala, Satun, Phang Nga and Krabi.

NORTHEAST REGION

Amnart Charoen, Bueng Kan, Buriram, Chaiyaphum, Loei, Mukdaharn, Khon Kaen, Udonthani, Mahasarakam, Kalasin, Nakhon Phanom, Nakhon Ratcha Si Ma, Nong Bua Lumpu, Nong Khai, Roi Et, Sakhon Nakhon, Si Saketh, Surin, Ubon Ratchathani, Yasothon.

BANGKOK

The actual name of Bangkok is listed in Guinness World Records as the world's longest place name at 168 letters;

"Krungthepmahanakhon Amornrattanakosin Mahintharayutthaya Mahadilokphop Nopparat Ratchathani Bureerom Udomratchanivwate Mahasathan Amornpiman Ourtan Satith Sakkathatiya Wisanu Khamprasit".

Bangkok or "Krungthep Mahanakorn" or "The City of Angels" was established as the capital of Thailand since 1782 in the reign of King Rama 1st

Its location is on the eastern side of the Chao Phraya River bank. The other side is called Thonburi; the former capital city during King Taksin period, but it's already gathered to Bangkok Administration and become now as one of the districts.

It occupies about 606 square miles with population of more than 10 millions.

BANGKOK METROPOLITAN

BANGKOK, NONTHABURI, NAKONPATHOM, PATHUMTHANI, SAMUTPRAKAN, SAMUTSAKON

Figure 28 Map of Bangkok Metropolitan

THE BANGKOK METROPOLITAN REGION

Bangkok and its borders are six provinces; namely started from the north, **Pathumthani, Nonthaburi, Chachoeng sao, Samutprakan, Samutsakon and Nakhonpathom.With the** exception of Chachoengsao, these provinces and Bangkok are formed The Bangkok Metropolitan Region.

When you visit Bangkok, you have to look around with other provinces nearby. You can only travel by public buses, sky trains, subways, cars, and taxi and tuk tuk.

Suwannaphum Airport located in Samutprakan, the province where is called "Paknam" or the mouth of The Chao Phraya River which flows to the Gulf of Thailand.

Figure 29 Bangkok Metropolitan; Bangkok, Nakonpathom, Nonthaburi, Samutprakan, Samutsakon and Pathumthani

EXPLORE BANGKOK

THE GRAND PALACE AND WAT PHRA KAEW

Visit **The Grand Palace**, the landmark of Thailand, and admire The Temple of Emerald Buddha.

(By MRT: at Sanamchai Station)

The Grand Palace; was established in 1782 in the reign of King Rama I, situated in Bangkok; the capital city since that time. The reason for choosing this capital because Thonburi; the former capital, was not suitable; with the river passing through the center of city, would be easily attacked. The other reason was; Thonburi Palace had two temples on each side, so the palace was located within a limited areas. King Rama I then ordered to establish the new palace in Bangkok; on the east bank of the Chao Phraya River, the main river of Thailand.

The Palace was original divided into three parts; the outer wall, the middle wall and the inner wall. Fortifications were installed with 12 gates and 17 ramparts.

Nowadays, the Grand Palace is opened for public for two parts; the temple of The Emerald Buddha or **Wat Phra Kaew** and within the center wall palace areas. Please dress modestly and try to see all buildings opened for public. Some of the hall is opened only for some important occasions. If you visit here without a guide, you should get information about the special events.

Figure 30 The golden pagoda or Phra Sirattana Chedi and Phra Mondop

WAT PHRA KAEW

Wat Phra Kaew or The Temple of Emerald Buddha was established in 1782, in outer wall of the palace. The tradition of building temple inside the palace were done since Sukhothai Period; Wat Mahathart in Sukhothai Palace and Wat Phra Si Sanpeth in Ayutthaya Palace. The temples built inside the palaces are different from other temples in general because there's no monk stay in these temples. The temples situated in the palaces are for the king and queen and the royal family performs religious ceremonies.

STEPS FOR ADMIRING IN WAT PHRA KAEW AREAS:

❖ THE HERMIT SCULPTURE

The statue of this hermit figure for commemorating of the Thai Traditional Medicine; the statue made of bronze and ordered to create during King Rama III period, with a mortar for crushing the herbal medicine. (some beliefs about making a medicine in front of statue enhanced medicinal properties)

❖ THE MURAL PAINTINGS OF RAMAYANA EPIC.

The paintings are on the walls around the areas of the temple. It's an ancient epic of India; telling about the war between King Rama and Tossakanth. The paintings consist of 178 sections, done since King Rama I period, has been renovated many times to maintain the beauty of Thai arts.

Please start the Wat Phra Kaew Tour by walking along the mural paintings before seeing other place surroundings and then get inside the main hall at the middle of the temple before going inside the palace areas.

Figure 31 The Hermit at the entrance of Wat Phra Kaew

Figure 32 The Mural Painting of Ramayana at Wat Phra Kaew

❑ THE YAK GUARDIANS

The Yak Statues or the demon; a character from the Ramayana Epic, are six pairs guard the gates. The statues were built in the reign of King Rama III.

❖ THE GOLDEN PAGODA OR PHRA SIRATANA CHEDI

The pagoda was built in the reign of King Rama IV, about in 1855 for enshrining the Relics of Buddha. It was in Bell-Shape or Ceylonese Style.

❖ PHRA MONDOP OR SCRIPTURE HALL

The building was built in the reign of King Rama I for housing Buddhist Scripture.

❖ PRASAT PHRA THEP BIDON OR THE ROYAL PANTHEON

The Chakri dynasty former kings statues kept here, the place is opened to the public on special holiday; especially on April 6th every year and on the daya of some royal ceremonies, they will be announced for the public if it's opened.

Figure 33 Prast Phrathep Bidon, Wat Phra Kaew

❖ PHRA BUSSABOK

Phra Bussabok are four of small pillars with elephants around, seen each corner of the scripture hall.

❖ BELFRY or The Bell Tower

In the ancient time, people did not have clocks so the bell rung from the temple was like, the clock to let the people know the time; such as, it's for calling the monks for last meal time at 11.00 am., for chanting time early in the morning and evening, and some special events in the temple. The bell tower is found in every temple.

Figure 34 Belfry at Wat Phra Kaew

❖ **MODEL OF ANGOR WAT**
❖ **PHRA ASADHA MAHA CHEDI**

The Eight Prang Towers are standing on the east of the temple. Prang is as stupa which is for keeping the ashes of the respected people.

Figure 35 Prangs

❖ **HOR PHRA OR BUDDHA STATUES HALL**

There are many pavilions and halls being as Hor Phra around the areas.

❖ **PHRA VIHARN YOD**

The structure of the building is beautiful in the form of Thai crown decorated with Chinese porcelain.

❖ **THE ORDINATION HALL OR PHRA UBOSOTH OR THE CHAPEL OF THE EMERALD BUDDHA**

The large building at the middle of the temple is the ordination hall; the main hall where the Emerald Buddha is situated. You are not allowed to use cameras inside the hall and please kindly sit on the floor. (Please don't point the feet to the direction of Buddha)

❑ When you get inside the chapel, please find a place to sit (on the floor), try to find the front place facing the Buddha image. Photo is not allowed but you can take the picture outside the chapel.

Sitting inside the main hall and meditate a while will give you a surprising boost of mental power. Please try!

You can take photo of The Emerald Buddha from outside the hall.

Figure 36 The Emerald Buddha or Phra Kaew Morakot

❑ **The statue of the Emerald Buddha is** covered by costumes which is changed in three seasons; summer, rainy season and winter, by the king.

❑ The statue of the Emerald Buddha was carved from a block of jasper in the attitude of meditation. The height is 66 cms. And the width measured by the base is 48.3 cms. From the evidences; by regarding of workmanship which was about Northern Thai Sculpture, assumed that were made during 15th Century.

❑ The mural painting inside the Chapel of The Emerald Buddha represents the Buddhist cosmology and the enlightenment of Buddha.

Figure 37 Chakri Maha Prasat Hall

THE PALACE AREAS

❑ The small gate passing to the palace after the The Emerald Buddha Temple is to **PHRA MAHA MONTIEN GROUP; the grand residential areas. The palace was built since 1782; in the reign of King Phra Phuttha Yod Fa Chula Loke the Great, King Rama I for coronation ceremonies of Chakri Dynasty. It's been used every reign continuously.. They are 7 connecting buildings:**

- **Phra Thinang Amarin Winitchai Mahai Suraya Phiman; the first part of the** group you meet, which was built in the reign of King Rama I in 1782, was used as the audience hall where the king met his officers and the ambassadors. The hall now is used for state occasions such as; coronation ceremony, the king's birthday and other special occasions from the palace.
- **Phra Thinang Paisal Taksin; located next to the front part, Phra Thinang Amarin, was the place where the king met his people and the situation of important sculptures.**
- **Phra Thinang Chakrapat Phiman; the palace was the royal resident of King Rama I.**
- **Hor Phra Suralai Phiman; the hall for Buddha statues.**
- **Hor Phra Dhart Monthian; it's enshrined the remains of King Rama I-III.**
- **Phra Thinang Thepsatan Phiras and Phra Thinang Theppa – ars Philai are located at the east and the west of this** palace. It was the the birthplace of Princess Petcharat Ratchasuda; the daughter of King Rama VI, the only one of the royal family who was born in Maha Montien Group Palace.

HOR SASTRAKOM; a small building nearby Phrathinag Amarin, it was built in the reign of King Rama IV. It's a place for religious rituals every Buddhist Holy Day.

❑ **CHAKRI MAHA PRASAT HALL; the** middle building with three spires on the building built in the reign of King Rama V in 1877. The building was constructed in mixed styles of European (Victorian) and Thai architecture. Due to its distinctive architecture than other royal residences, The Chakri Maha Prasart Hall has now become one of the most important attractions of the Grand Palace. It was the royal resident for King Rama V during his reign.

The Chakri Maha Prasat Hall is now used as state banquets. This is a three-storey building built in "T" plan. The front building is divided into three parts; the east, the central and the west wings. The wings are connected by corridors.

❑ Visit the first floor of the Chakri Maha Prasat Hall, which is a museum for ancient weapons.

❑ **DUSIT MAHA PRASART HALL**; the hall has been admired for a great art masterpiece of Rattanakosin. It's the only hall in the grand palace built with authentic Thai architecture. It was built in the reign of King Rama I, with a very beautiful spired roof on the top. It's the last hall before you leave the palace.

This hall is for; lying-in-state of Kings, queens and members of the royal family, as a principal function. The hall was enshrined the body of His Majesty King Bhumibol; King Rama 9th about a year and we were allowed to come here for paying respect to his body during the funeral period in 2016-2017.

Figure 38 Left to right; Chakri Maha Prasat and Dusit Maha Prasat

You can walk along the wall of the palace to Wat Pho.

Figure 39 Wat Pho

WAT PHO

Wat Pho and the Grand Palace can be combined tour for one day trip, but if you don't have much time; you can have a quick look of each place inside Wat Pho. I would like you to visit this temple after when you visit the Grand Palace.

The location of Wat Pho is close to BTS Sanamchai Station and The Grand Palace. If you are tired after The Grand Palace tour, you can ride Tuk Tuk from the palace to Wat Pho.

The full name of Wat Pho is called "Wat Phra Chetupon Wimon Mungkhalaram" or known as The Temple of Reclining Buddha.

Wat Pho was the 24th most popular tourist destination in the world in 2006, with almost 9 millions visiting that year. The temple was one of the oldest temples in Bangkok but the year of building was unknown. It's where King Rama 1st rebuilt the temple complex sites to make it the royal temple. Wat Pho was renovated and expanded during King Rama III period.

Figure 40 The Pagodas at Wat Pho

EXPLORING WAT PHO

❑   See the statues of **Yak; Demon Guardian** statues at
the entrance.

❑   See the statues of **Chinese Guardians** beside the gate
to the The Hall of Reclining Buddha.

❑ See the Illustrations in the medicine pavilion. **Wat Pho** is known as the birthplace of Traditional Thai Massage and houses of Thai Medicine. The marble illustrations and inscriptions placed in the pavilion (along the way to the main hall) for public instructions have been registered by **UNESCO in its Memory of the World Programme in 2008. The temple still** remains a center for tradition medicine. You can try Thai traditional massage here.

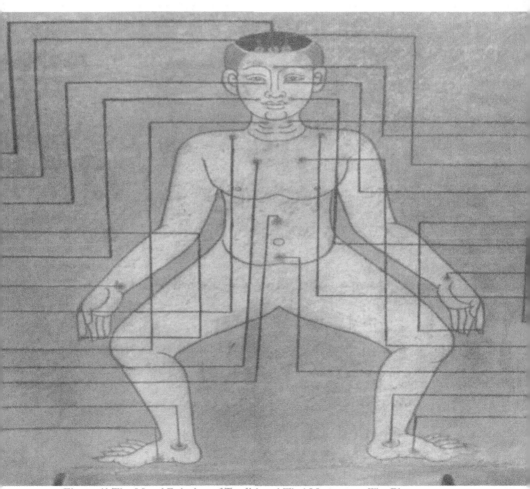

Figure 41 The Mural Painting of Traditional Thai Massage at Wat Pho

Figure 42 The Reclining Buddha at Wat Pho

❑ **See the Hall of Reclining Buddha which** is at the west of the temple near Chao Phraya River. The hall was built in the reign of King Rama III for covering the statue of the Reclining Buddha. The colorful mural painting inside the hall depicts about the outstanding Buddhists; for Phikkhu, Phikkhunee, Ubasoke and Ubasika; called as Athatakkha.

❑ **The beautiful Reclining Buddha was made of stucco** cladded with gold sheets all over the statue; which is 46 meter long and 15 meter high, the 3rd largest reclining Buddha in Thailand.

❏ Walk around inside the hall and admire this beautiful Reclining Buddha image. See the soles of the feet which are in laid with mother-of-pearl display 108 auspicious symbols of Buddha.

❏ You will hear the sounds of coins hitting the monks' bowl when you enter the hall. They are 108 bowls for people to drop the coins; it's like a donation for the temple; some people believe that they are offering to 108 monk alms.

❏ When you leave the hall, you will see the beautiful huge pagodas or Phra Mahachedi of the four kings. You can get inside this part to see more of buildings.

❏ **See Phra Mondop;** a square building with spire roof decorated with porcelains near the huge pagodas.

❏ **Sala Kan Pa Riean;** the large hall nearby the stupas.

When you finish the part of the Reclining Buddha, you should walk to the main hall or the ordination hall areas. You will see lots of stupas along the way around the temples.

❑ See the interior of **The Ordination Hall** having the beautiful Principal Buddha Statue on a top base. The Buddha statue was brought from other temple by King Rama I and the image was built in meditation position. **The Viharns** or small pavilions of four directions are situated with the Buddha Statues along the cloister around the ordination hall.

❑ See the statue **of hermits in 24** positions around in the temple areas; in fact, there were about 80 statues of hermits in different positions with descriptions of each position, but some of the statues were destroyed and stolen, then only 24 left.

Figure 43 Hermits in 24 positions at Wat Pho

Figure 44 Phra Maha Chedi of the four kings

❑ **Phra Maha Chedi (Pagoda) of the four kings**; King Rama 1st -4th , which built for worshipping to Buddha, are large pagodas located next to the Reclining Buddha Hall surrounded by walls. The architecture around the arch was Thai- Chinese style. The pagodas are decorated with glazed tiles. There is a pair of Chinese stone dolls decorated on each door.

Figure 45 The stupas and Chinese doll

Figure 46 Phra Mondop at Wat Pho with Yak Guardians at the door

❑ Wat Pho has the most pagodas in Thailand. There are **99 pagodas and** stupas in the temple area; the 71 small stupas around built in the reign of King Rama 3rd for containing the ashes of the royal family, The 20 pagoda along the cloister; 5 ones of each corner contain Buddha's Relic and the 4 Phra Maha Stupas; Prang style; like corn shape, are outside the ordination hall.

After exploring Wat Pho, you should walk around long the river-bank and find something to drink and eat in a small restaurant nearby the temple or just go to the Tha Maharaj.

There are two piers close to The Grand Palace, **Tha Chang and Tha Maharaj** Piers. There are many nice places at Tha Maharaj Pier; which located next to Tha Chang Pier, take a break before moving further more places.

Figure 47 Ferry Boat cost about 3 Bahts for crossing The Chao Phraya River

Figure 48 Wat Mahathat

❑ Walk along the road in front of the palace to see more places such as; Sanam Luang Ground, the Bangkok City Pillar, Ministry of Defense, The Bangkok National Museum, Wat Mahathat and Thammasat University.

❑ Visit **Wat Mahathat; which** is the center of the Buddhist Mahanikai School, originally built to house Buddha's relic. The temple is opposite to Tha Maharaj Pier. Walk along the pathways and see old shops for local street food and herbs.

❑ See **Thammasat University** near Tha Phra Chan Pier; next from Tha Maharaj Pier. It's a state university, the 2nd oldest university since 1934.

❑   If you walk along the pathway near the river, you will discover the market of the Thai Buddha amulets for "votive tablet" or blessed statue of Buddha image at **Tha Phra-Chan Pier.**

❑   Enjoy the typical Thai restaurants of old time along the small lane nearby the riverside of Ta Phra- Chan Pier. One of my favorite restaurants here is Café 79"s. must try!

❑   Visit **MUSEUM SIAM** at Sanam Chai Road near Wat Pho. The museum of Thai Historical exhibitions.

❑   Stand on the ground of Sanam Luang; the large ground areas facing The Grand Palace, which is the historic center for the Royal Ceremonies. Nice location to take picture of The Grand Palace areas here.

When I was young, I came to see the Kite Flying Festival at Sanam Luang when trade winds flew. People brought their beautiful kites to flow in the sky.

Kite Flying was a traditional sport since Sukhothai Period (1238-1438) and has been very popular for Thai people. King Rama IV allowed people to play kite-flying at Sanam Luang or called as "Thung Phra Main". The event has been held during February-April for once a year together with many activities performed and exhibitions of Thai arts.

Sanam Luang Ground was the rice field in the ancient time. It's the site for royal ceremonies and for the cremation of kings and queens. Nowadays, it's listed as a historical site.

Figure 49 Sanam Luang and The Royal Cremetorium of King Bhumibol

Figure 50 Tuktuk, Wat Mahathat, Bangkok City Pillar and Bangkok Museum

❑ See The Bangkok City Pillar Shrine at the corner of street in front of the palace ground. The City Pillar Shrines or Lak Mueng is found every province in Thailand. Lak Mueng came from ancient traditions; Brahman's customs believed that it's the center of soul for citizens and needed to be respected to the guardian's spirit here.

❏ Walk around the Grand Palace Fortifications and see a beautiful yellow old building which is the Ministry of Defense.

❏ See **The Bangkok National Museum;** from Sanam Luang Ground, you can see the museum is situated by the street in front of Sanam Luang.

❏ Ride a ferry boat across the river at Tha Phra Chan near Thammasat University to Tha Wang Lang Pier; the west bank of The Chao Phraya River where located near Siriraj Hospital, one of the best medical center in Thailand.

❏ Try street food nearby the Tha Wang Lang Pier and enjoy walking along the food vendors.

❏ See **Siriraj Hospital**, one of the state hospitals in Thailand, it's the primary teaching hospital of the faculty of Medicine Siriraj Hospital of Mahidol University. The hospital was founded by King Rama V (King Chularongkorn) in 1888. It was the resident of King Bhumibol (Rama 9th) for treatment in between 2009-2013 and he died here in Oct13, 2016. You can visit museums inside the hospital which exhibits history of medicine in Thailand from traditional to modern medicine.

The location of hospital is surrounded by many old buildings and much street food at the opposite side. Explore the areas by walking through the small lanes.

Figure 51 The large bells in front of Wat Rakang

Figure 52 The statue of Luang Por Tho at wat Rakang

WAT RAKANG

❑ Enjoy walking around and pass through a narrow lane which led to **Wat Rakhang Kositaram** or called as Wat Rakhang or "Wat Luang Por Tho".

The temple is one of the old temples of Ayutthaya Period. "Rakhang" means "Bell", so you can see a huge bell on the front ground of the temple. From the temple's historical background, an old bell was found in the temple ground during restoration in the reign of King Rama I. This bell was moved to Wat Phra Kaew and the king ordered to make 5 more bells for Wat Rakhang.

- ❑ Admire a beautiful principal Buddha or called as "Luang Por Yim"; "Yim" means "Smile", inside the ordination hall of Wat Rakhang. King Rama V visited the temple for religious ceremony and appreciated the statue and then he named the Buddha Statue as "Phra Yim Rub Fah"; means the principal Buddha smiles to everyone who enters the hall.

- ❑ At the Wat Rakhang Pier is situated a huge Monk Statue of Luang Por Toh; or Somdet Toh (1788-1872); he was one of the most famous and well respected monk in Thailand, his statues are seen nationwide in the temples and his amulets; which believed that the Buddha amulets are full of supernatural power, are sought among all worshippers. He was an abbot of Wat Rakhang during King Rama IV-V period. People come here for paying homage to his statue and have a chance for evening-chanting with the monks in the late afternoon.

- ❑ Admire a beautiful unique Scripture Halls of Wat Rakhang (near an old Phra Viharn Hall)

- ❑ From Wat Rakang, you can ride a boat to Wat Arun and followed by Wat Kalayanamit. But if you come from Icon Siam Pier, you will see Wat Kalayanamit firstly. There are boat tour for 3 temples; Wat Rakang, Wat Arun and Wat Kalayanamit, from the taxi boats.

❑   **Wat Kalayanamit** is located next to Wat Rakang. It was built in the reign of King Rama III. You can come here from Pak Klong Talat Pier by ferry boat or come from Wat Arun. The temple is famous for the the principal Buddha image which built in "Pa Leh Lai" attitude and the mural painting of the ordination hall were described the picture of "Doctor Bradley" and his raft house.

"Phra Pang Pa Leh Lai" is the image of Buddha built in sitting position on a stone, the feet on the lotus, the right hand is turned upward on his right knee and the left hand is turned downward on his left knee, with an elephant statue kneeled down with a pail of water in its trunk and a monkey statue carried honeycomb for offering to the Buddha.

Doctor Bradley or Dan Beach Bradley was an American Protestant missionary who traveled to Siam in 1835 and lived until his death. He brought the first Thai-script printing press to Siam for publishing the first newspaper, performed the first surgery and introduced the western medicine and technology to Siam.

Figure 53 Wat Arun

WAT ARUN OR
THE TEMPLE OF DAWN

I usually ride a boat from Wat Rakhang to Wat Arun or **THE TEMPLE OF DAWN**. The temple looks so beautiful not only at dawn but also at night. If you join the dinner cruise tour, you will see the lights on the pagoda image with other small pagodas surround. It's a nice shot from the Chao Phraya River. You can come here directly by **MRT** at Itsaraphap Station; exit 2 and walk about **15 minutes**.

❑ Going to The Temple of Dawn can be done from Wat Pho or The Grand Palace by river boats from the 4 piers; Tha Tien, Tha Chang, Tha Maharaj and Tha Phra Chan, or ride MRT to Issaraphap Station exit 2 and walk for 10 mins.

"Tha" comes from the word "Tha Rue" means "Pier"

❑ **The Temple of Dawn** was an old temple since Ayutthaya Period. The former name is called Wat Chaeng; "Chaeng" means "Clearly Seen:" It was a royal temple during King Taksin built his palace to be close to the temple.

The temple and the stunning pagoda were renovated since King Rama I-IV period. The stunning huge Phra Prang is now the landmark for Thonburi City; the west bank of The Chao Phraya River.

❑ **Admire a very beautiful pagoda or Phra Prang Wat Arun from the boat ride. Phra Prang Wat Arun** is the highest Prang Tower in Thailand and a symbol of Tourism Authority of Thailand.

The Temple of Dawn joined the special event on St. Patrick's Day; The Global Greening Programme 2021, at 19.00 Pm., the Huge Phra Prang went green.

❏ Phra Prang or the huge pagoda situated nearby the river-bank is surrounded by 4 Prangs. The original size of Phra Prang was only 16 meter high built since Ayutthaya period. It was rebuilt in 1842 and renovated as it's seen nowadays in the reign of King Rama V period about in 1909. The height is 81.85 meters. The pagoda is made of brick covered with plaster with the decorations of colorful porcelains from China into Angels, Yak and Phaya Krut (or a mystical bird) images on the pagoda.

❑ The temples and city tours for one day trip are The Grand Palace and Wat Pho in the morning and have lunch at Tha Maharaj or Tha Phra Chan then continues with Wat Rakang, Wat Arun and Wat Kalayanamit by ferry boat, taxi boat or the routine express boat. Hang out at Tha Wang Lang and back to Wat Mahathat. Enjoy the scenery of Sanam Luang and continue to explore Ratchadamnoen Avenue.

If you have time or stay at Khaosan road, you can ride the boat to Tha Phra Artit which full of café and restaurants. The areas are known as the old style city areas where it was the locations of many palaces since King Rama IV period. You can also enjoy the walkway along the Chao Phraya River, viewing the nice scenery of Rama 8th Bridge. It's nice to think of the old days here whenever we sit and relax awhile near the river. I recommend Tha Phra Artit.

Figure 54 Wat Arun at sunset

RATCHA DAM NOEN AVENUE

Figure 55 The Democracy Monument

❑ Walk along **Ratcha-dam-noen Avenue**, the historic road in Bangkok, the main road is where some old buildings and temples are seen. You can ride taxi or Tuk Tuk for looking around after the Grand Palace tour. You will pass by this avenue before going to the Marble Temple which located near the Equestrain Statue of King Chularlongkorn the Great or King Rama V. But if you would like to explore places around the street areas, you can walk and ride taxi or tuk tuk to see the monuments, Wat Saketh, Wat Ratchanadda and Wat Suthat with the Giant Swing.

- See the **Democracy Monument; situated on Ratcha Dam Noen Avenue,** which was commissioned in 1939 to commemorate of "Siamese Revolution of 1932"
- See The Equestrain Statue of King Rama V **and The Ananta Samakhom Throne Hall**; The Reception Hall for the king at The Dusit Palace, on Ratchadamnoen Avenue.

Figure 56 The Equestrain Statue of King Rama V

WAT SA KETH

❑ Visit **Wat Sa Keth**; or called as a Golden Mount Temple where you can view a picturesque Bangkok of old areas on Rat chadamnoen Avenue. The golden pagoda is seen when you pass by Ratchadamnoen Avenue. It's an old temple since Ayutthaya period which located near Klong Mahanak Canal. It's known of the sacred big pagoda on the top of a little hill and the story legend told about the "Vulture of Wat Saketh"

Figure 57 Phu Khao Thong at Wat Sa Keth

❑ The Pagoda on the hilltop; a model of a hill constructed in the temple for pagoda, was built in the reign of King Rama IV in 1865, contained Buddha's relic. The height is 59 meters or equal to 19 storey-building. You can climb the staircases to the top to view the Bangkok city.

"**Raeng at Wat Saketh**" ; Raeng means Vulture, has been the famous legend of the vultures at Wat Saketh which was told when the Cholera spreaded all over Thailand during King Rama III period in 1820 and about 30,000 people died in the capital. Wat Saketh was the main place for receiving the dead bodies. The temple was unable to cremate all the bodies that moved here, so many of them left in the open areas and devoured by many vultures. It's a common told-story when we talked about Wat Saketh and the vultures of old time.

WAT RATCHANADDARAM

❏ Wat Ratchanaddaram is the temple located opposite to Wat Sa Keth at the corner near Mahakan Fort. This temple is one of the archaeological sites where **The Loha Prasat**; the only one Buddhist Steel Castle left in the world, It was built in the reign of King Rama III about 180 years ago. The beautiful Thai arts of this Loha Prasat are 3-storey building with 37 spire-roofs. The buildings were renovated in 2015 by cladding gold leaves on Mondops at the 2nd and 3rd floor.

Figure 58 Wat Ratchanadda; Loha Prasart, King RamaIII Statue and the golden mountain nearby.

WAT BENJAMABORPIT OR THE MARBLE TEMPLE

❑ The Marble Temple or Wat Benjamaborpit was constructed in 1899 during King Rama V period. It's close to The Dusit Palace; his palace.

❑ Admire the beautiful front of the Ordination Hall when you enter the temple. This is the main building of the temple, courtyard and lion sculpture are made of marble from Italy; Carrara Marble. The image of the temple' façade is on Thai 5 -Baht Coin.

You can get inside the hall for admiring the beautiful statue Buddha image and the photo of King Chularlongkorn or King Rama V during his monkhood and see some decorations inside the hall.

❑ **The beautiful Sukhothai Art of Principal Buddha Image is called Phra Phuttha** Chinnaraj; built in 1920, a copy of the original one in Phitsanulok Province. Within the base of the Buddha Statue are the ashes of King Rama V buried.

The interior of the ordination hall; the main hall, decorated with lacquer and gold in paintings of all important pagodas of Thailand and some colorful stained glasses above the windows are beautiful when it's shone in the light.

The cloister around the hall houses 52 images of Buddha in different attitudes.

Early in the morning, people come to the temple for offering to the monks' alms and meditate in the hall. The monk preaches in the hall during Buddha's Day and the hall may be full of people, but you can still get inside here.

WAT TRIMITH

❑ Travel to Wat Trimit can do by MRT: Hualumphong Statation; **THE HUA LUM PHONG RAILWAY STATION IS HERE, and walk to Trimit** Road for visiting Wat Trimit or The Golden Buddha Temple. When I was a tourguide, I started the temple tour from Wat Trimit because it's easy to continue Wat Pho by passing Yaowaraj.

❑ Wat Trimith is one of the oldest temples located nearby Yaowaraj Road or China Town Areas. The former name was Wat "Sam Chin" which means "three Chinese"; assumed that built by the three Chinese which were friends. In 1934, the temple was restored by the former abbot and after that the temple was named "Wat Trimith" in 1939. The areas of this temple consist of the religious rituals ground and schools; for monks and public school. People come here for the Golden Buddha.

Figure 59 The Chapel of the Golden Buddha

Figure 60 The front of Wat Trimit

Figure 61 Phra Sukhothai Trimit or the Golden Buddha

❑ Phra Sukhothai Trimit; the golden Buddha Statue is the biggest golden Buddha statue in the world, the height is 3.91 meters and the width is 3.01 meters, made of solid gold weigh 5.5 tons.

❑ The Buddha was original covered with stucco and unknown about the origins; but from the art of sculpture, the sculpture would be the style of Sukhothai during 13th Century.

The statue was original covered with stucco and situated outdoor at Wat Phraya Krai near the Chao Phraya River before. It was assumed that the golden statue was covered to protect the gold and prevent from stealing; especially, preventing the enemies during the war.

The Buddha Statue was moved to Wat Trimit and situated outdoor nearby the road for 20 years because of the huge size. The plaster was clacked in 1955 during moving the statue for situating inside the new hall and the gold appeared. The abbot ordered for removing all the plasters from the statue. The plasters covering the statue are displayed to the public in the temple.

❑ King Rama 9th ordered to build a new Mondop Building; a square building with spire-roof, covering the Buddha Statue in 2007 for The King's 80th Birthday Celebration.

Figure 62 Yaowaraj Road

- ❏ You can view the Yaowaraj Road from the top of the chapel.
- ❏ Walk along the small alleys of the China Town from <u>Wat Trimit</u>. (Get some nice Thai-Chinese food at the opposite side of the temple such as noodles, rice with grilled pork pour with sweet sauce or "Khow Moo Dang" and Pad Thai I recommend!
- ❏ Enjoy walking along **Yaowaraj Road** (about 1.5 kilometers) in the China Town area. If you ride the subway, MRT: Wat Mangkorn Station is the destination to explore China Town; the amazing markets which are full of everything you need, especially delicious food.
- ❏ Enjoy walking along small lanes in **Pahurat Market** or Indian Market which is not so far from Yaowaraj; it's where you can find fabric shops, delicious Indian food and cheap accessories. BTS: at Samyod Station or Wat Mangkorn Station. Walking here is fun!
- ❏ Fun Kayaking along The Klong Ong Ang; the canal at the center of Bangkok within the areas of The China Town and Indian Market, to see a Street of Art and experience the hostels nearby and enjoy variety of much Indian food.

THE GIANT SWING

Figure 63 Wat Suthat and the Giant Swing

❑ See the **Giant Swing** and walk around the street of religious supplier shops near the Bangkok Metropolitan Administration.

THE GIANT SWING; was built in 1784 and renovated many times, the swing is situated on the stone base with its height of 21.15 meters. The Swing Ceremony was a part of Hindu Rituals performed and celebrated here for until the reign of King Rama VII then it was cancelled because of accidents. Nowadays, the rituals are performed inside the shrine only.

Figure 64 The Giant Swing and Bangkok Administration Office

Walk around the Giant Swing areas for nice food and see many old buildings which are commercial buildings and residential areas.

Figure 65 Wat Suthat

WAT SUTHAT

❑ Visit **Wat Suthat; a beautiful temple in front of the Giant Swing,** built in 1807. This is where King Rama 8th Monument situated.

❑ Admire many beautiful architectures and sculptures inside **Wat Suthat** temple such as; the ordination hall which is the longest size in Thailand; 72.25 meter long and 22.60 meter wide, the principal Buddha image in the hall, the large Phra Viharn of about 24meter wide and 27 meter long which is amazing; with Thai style decorations and the outstanding painting on the doors (front and back) painted by King Rama II., Chinese dolls and look around the sculptures.

❑ See many religious supplier-shops around the areas of The Giant Swing.

❑ Try some Thai food from a small restaurants and street vendors at night here. If you walk along Mahachai Rd., you will see old famous restaurants for Phad Thai (Thipsamai) and Je Phai restaurant. The street vendors come during sunset.

I think if you choose to visit within these areas, you need one day trip by starting Wat Saketh, Wat Ratchanadda, Wat Suthat and the Giant Swing areas. I always enjoy here indeed.

❑ Walk around **Bobae Market**, the big wholesale and retail shopping areas, and the cheap clothing market. MRT: at Hua Lumphong Station and connect the local bus no. 53.

• Visit **Pak Klong Talat or the Flower** Market by River boat. The name of the pier here is called Pak Klong Talat; where you can cross the river to Wat Kalayanamit.

❑ Ride a river boat to **ICON SIAM**; one of the largest shopping malls in Asia. You can ride a river boat to anywhere from this mall.I like this mall because it's large and nice to walk inside the mall. I usually enjoy the food at the ground floor; many kinds of delicious food with reasonable prices. There are 5 star hotels located nearby this mall. The skytrain to Icon Siam Station is also convenient to visit other parts of Bangkok.

❑ You can ride the shuttle boat to enjoy **Asiatique the River Front. It's a place full of shops and restaurants.The** free shuttle boats are from **Sathorn Pier** near Taksin Bridge. BTS: Saphan Taksin Station. You can enjoy **The Calypso Cabaret Show** at Asiatique River Front and dinner. For those who like to enjoy the show from her male, you should not miss here.

Taksin Hospital is located near Icon Siam. It's one of the old hospitals in Thailand, established in 1904. "Taksin" came from the name of the king of Thonburi Capital. The location of the hospital is not so far from the King Taksin the Great Memorial at Wong Wien Yai Circle. On December 28th every year is recognized as King Taksin's Day. The present king with the royal family will come to lay the wreaths at the monument. People also come to this memorial for laying flowers for expressing their gratitude to King Taksin the Great for his brave fighting with Burmese Army and brought freedom back to Siam and established Thonburi to be the capital.

Figure 66 The Royal Barge during the royal ceremony in front of the palace.

❏ Admire **National Museum of The Royal Barges** of collection of 8 royal barges in Thonburi side by speed boat. The Royal Barges are still used during The Royal Barge Procession on the most significant cultural and religious events. You can come here by ferry boat from Bangkok Noi Train Station here. If you are close to Siriraj Hospital, you can walk here.

❏ **Join the Floating market tours in Bangkok, at Klong Lat Mayom and Taling Chan Foating Markets by speed boat. They are beautiful floating markets in Bangkok.**

Figure 67 The Royal Barge Museum

☐ Enjoy **Dinner Cruise; if you are** during Loy Krathong Day Festival, you will enjoy the beautiful Fireworks and the lighted candles are glittery on all decorated banana-leaf baskets floating on the river. It's a Full Moon Day after Buddhist Lent Day. It's a fantastic night.

☐ Exploring canals by speed boat to see the "Venice of the east" in areas of Thonburi river-bank side by speed boat.

☐ Discover **Talat Nam Klong Bangluang;** it's a floating market in Thonburi where the many old wooden houses along the canal still preserved as the olden days. You can hire the speed boat to explore.

☐ Enjoy walking around **"Chang Chui",** the amazing shops and artworks of unlimited arts and creations. MRT: Sirindhorn Station.

❑ The old Chinese Mansion **"Lhong 1919"** and the old styles of the Chinese resident areas, located opposite to Talat Noi Pier are now closed since Dec1, 2021.

When you are in Thonburi District, you have to visit the wellknown temple with Big Buddha image located by Phasi Jaroen Canal. The boat trip along this canal is fascinating; full of beautiful temples and one of the popular and very famous temples is Wat Paknam Phasi Jaroen.

WAT PAKNAM PHASI JAROEN

Figure 68 The Pagoda of Buddha's Relic on the top floor of Phra Maha Chedi at Wat Paknam

Wat Paknam was established in about 1610 during Ayutthaya period. It locates near Phasi jaroen Canal. You can go to this temple by MRT and get off at Bang Phai Station, but you have to walk along the narrow road of Phetkasem Soi 23 to reach the temple. I think you should get a taxi for about 40 Bahts here rather than by walking. The temple is well organized with many large buildings includes a huge Stupa and the large Buddha Statue.

The stupa or called as Phra Maha Chedi is 80 meter high with five floors; the 2nd floor is a museum of Buddhist items includes the Buddha statues collected from old time, the 3rd floor has the Luang Por Sod statue; the former abbot and the 4th floor has a beautiful pagoda of Buddha's Relic. You can admire the views and a large Buddha statue from the 3rd floor.Must see the Big Buddha; Phra Phuttha Dhammakai Thepmongkon; which is as tall as 20th floor building, with 69 meter high and 40 meter wide built in 2017 to honor Luang Pu Sod and the Royal family. Luang Pu Sod was the former abbot who widely known for starting "Dhammakai Meditation" method.

Figure 69 The Big Buddha and The Pagoda

Figure 70 Get closer to the Big Buddha on the third floor

he old corner and Chinese temple at Talat No

Figure 71 Talat Noi

- ❑ Experience a traditional Chinese quarter at **Talat Noi,** a cultural attractions with several historic buildings from 300 years ago. (By the River Boat with orange flag, stop at Ta-Krom-Chao-ta or say "Talat Noi")
- ❑ **Hire a bicycle for roaming around Talat Noi areas.**
- ❑ Admire The Kalawa Church near Talat Noi.
- ❑ Admire the old aged Chinese Temples/ God's Shrine in Talat Noi.
- ❑ Taste a popular stir-fried noodle dish and famous curry puffs at Talat Noi.
- ❑ Admire the streets of art at Talat Noi.
- ❑ Try the local coffee and charcoal grilled breads at Talat Noi.

Figure 72 Jatujak Market

JATUJAK MARKET

❑ Shop at **Jatujak Market** near the Jatujak Park and eat at Or Tor Kor Market Food Court, opposite to the Jatujak Park. (BTS: at Morchit Station, MRT: at Kham Phaeng Peth Station) The market is opened about 6 am-6 pm during weekend. You can check the schedule for accurate time when you are in Thailand. There are thousands of shops and vendors here. It's the world's largest weekend market with crowded every weekend. You can find anything in Jatujak Market.

❑ Enjoy walking around **Soi Aree** street food the community mall. (BTS: at Aree Station)

❑ Shop at the **Central Plaza Ladprow** and enjoy the restaurants of international food. Nice to walk here.
 BTS: at Ha Yak Lad-prow Station,
 MRT: at Pha-hol-yo-thin Station.
❑ Watch a movie **at Major Cineplex** and enjoy eating the varieties of food from many restaurants and a night market. (BTS: at Ratchayothin Station)
❑ Experience **Bang Sue Grand Railway** Station near Jatujak Park, the largest railway station in Southeast Asia with 26 platforms about 600 meters long, and ride the train for sight-seeing.

Figure 73 Victory Monument

VICTORY MONUMENT

❑ Walk around the area of **Victory Monument**, the gate to downtown in Bangkok. If you come by Airport Link, stop at Phayathai Station; from here, you can choose where to go easily; connect BTS: to **Siam Station; the main station to go other places;** at Siam Station you will find Siam Paragon Shopping Mall and others, or go direct to Samut Prakan Province for The Erawan Museum, etc. You can also catch a train to Phahonyothin route for visit the northeast of Bangkok areas from Phayathai.

Figure 74 Traffic jam on Yaowaraj Rd.

❑ Walk along the sky Bridge from Siam to World Trade Center and see Ratchaprasong Square. (BTS: at Siam) When you reach here, you can go to Pratunam; the local market for street vendors and The Platinum Mall; the wholesales fabric and goods. If you ride the skytrain from the airport, you can get off at Ratchaprarop Station and walk to Pratunam.

❑ The skytrain from Siam can go up to Samutprakan Province where there are many attractions. Please see the details of Samutprakan.

FOUR- FACE GOD SHRINE OR ERAWAN SHRINE

❑ Admire the **Erawan Shrine; which is called as Four–face God Shrine from tourists,** often features performances by Thai Dance troupes hired by the worshippers who succeeded in what they wished. The statue is situated at the corner of Ratchaprasong Square.

❑ Visit the **Bangkok Art and Culture Center;** a very interesting contemporary arts center of art education with book shop, library and commercial art galleries. It also aims for cultural exchange. (BTS: at the National Stadium Station)

The national stadium is called Suphachalasi Stadium; the sport complex in Bangkok. It's established in 1937 and expanded for multiple stadia and sport facilities. I came to this stadium for watching Michael Jackson Concert in 1993 which was open-air at the football field.I had much fun in the past.

❑ Fun walking and shop around **Siam Square** and enjoy many activities at Siam **Paragon, Siam Center, Siam Discovery.**

❑ Walking around the **Maboonklong** Shopping Mall (big mobile market), you have to be careful of your bags during walking in this area when it's crowded.   BTS: at Siam Station

Maboonklong locates near The National Stadium.

There is a park called **Lumpini Park** near the MTR Station at Silom where you can relax and exercise. It's near Chulalongkorn Hospital; a state hospital and very well organized for medical service. If your accommodation is close to Silom Rd., Sathon Rd., Ploenchit Rd. and nearby Hua Lumphong railway station, you can come to the park easily by sky train (BTS: Saladaeng) Jog and walk and then go to explore Silom Road.

Figure 75 Lumpini Park

LUMPINI PARK

❑ Enjoy jogging and relax at Lumpini Park, the big park in the center of Bangkok, for recreations and exercises. It is the lung of Bangkok people. I love here in the morning time but afternoon time is also good. It's a fun workout here!

- Walk on King Power **Mahanakorn Skywalk;** the largest Glass Tray Observation deck for 360 degrees panoramic view, the highest rooftop in Bangkok. (BTS: at Chongnonsee Station) It's located on Silom Road which is not so far from Lumpini Park.
- Enjoy looking around **Samyan Midtown** by MRT : Samyan exit 2
- Walk around **the Commons Community** Mall. (BTS: at Thong Lor Station)
- Shopping at night in the Ratchada Local Night Market or **Train Market** or "Talat Rodfai". (MRT: at Rat-chada Station) It's like a flea market for many things; sold from vendors who bring their own products and food. It's a popular place for people after work.

Figure 76 Talat Rodfai, Train Market

JIM THOMSON HOUSE

Figure 77 Jim Thomson House

❑ Visit **Jim Thomson House**; a museum which houses the Southeast Asian art collections; especially the Buddha Statues in many styles of art. The building is a typical Thai architectural style; received the Architectural Conservation Award in 1996.

Jim Thomson; the owner of Jim Thomson House, was an American business man and famous for Thai Silk business in Thailand. He was disappeared mysteriously when he was 61 years old in 1967.

❑ See **Khlong Saen Saep**; a canal nearby Jim Thomson House, one of the canal for public transports (express boats) service in the center of Bangkok. The length of the canal is 72 kms passing many districts and connected to small canals. Riding a boat to see the local living life style by canals. Rush hour is in between 7-9 am and 4-6 pm.

❑ Experience a night life of **Soi Cowboy in** Nana Plaza. It's one of the Red-light districts in Bangkok. (BTS: at Nana Station)

❑ Experience nightlife of **Soi Pat Pong areas**; one of the Red-light districts in Bangkok. (BTS: at Saladaeng Station)

The Red-light districts are places of bars, go-go bars, clubs and restaurants. There are some street vendors for goods and food. Please use discretion during walking around in these areas. You may only walk through with friends or your companions. Ladies should avoid walking alone in this area.

KHAOSAN ROAD

❑ Roaming around the streets **at Khaosan** Road, popular places for backpackers, a nightlife spot in Bangkok. There are buses from Suwannaphum Airport to Khaosan. When you stay at the guesthouses or hotels at Khoasan Rd., you can visit **Wat Chanasongkram**, Wat Bowonniweth Ratchavoraviharn and the old market called **Banglumpoo.**

❑ **Wat Bowonniweth Ratchavoraviharn** is the temple where the former abbots stayed and the first Monk's College called Mahamakut Buddhist University located. You can admire the two beautiful Buddha images in the hall.

WAT INTHARAVIHARN

❑ From Khaosan Road, you can walk to Wat Intharaviharn; the famous temple where the huge standing Buddha situated. The statue is 32 meter high built in 1867 by Luang Por Tho (the former abbot of Wat Rakang) in the reign of King Rama IV but finished in the reign of King Rama VII, the standing Buddha was named "Phra Puttasi Ariya Mettrai"; the statue contains Buddha's relic on the head of this Buddha image. Must see!

Figure 78 Luang Por Tho at Wat Intharaviharn

❑ Discover the **Airplane Graveyard** on Ramkamhaeng Road 103 alley, the abandoned 747 and two smaller MD-82 planes lying in pieces becoming homes of the families. (Airport Link: at Ramkamhaeng Station and ride a taxi there. Ramkamhaeng areas are the rural side of Bangkok at Bangkapi District. Not much to see, but if you really have many days only for Bangkok, you may like to experience here.

❑ Admire the **big green Jade Buddha** statue at **Wat Dhammamongkol** on Sukhumvit Road 101 alley. (BTS: at Pun-na-withi Station) When you get off the train here, get a taxi or local tuktuk to the temple.

❑ Enjoy **The Siam Niramit** Show; the traditional Thai dance and drama performed on stage include with dinner package.

❑ "**KHON**" is a Thai traditional dance, performed on stage with masks; the expressing characteristics of Dancers in the drama based on the ancient epic; Ramayana. The Thai traditional shows at the dinner tour mostly perform dancing and wear costumes like Khon.

❑ Enjoy **The Safari World;** the open zoo of Safari Park and Marine Park with special shows, one of the tourist attractions in Bangkok. (it's not so far from the airport)

❑ Enjoy **The Wonder World Fun Park** opposite to the **Fashion Island** shopping malls; a nice mall for walking around. (nearby Suwannaphum Airport)

❑ Enjoy **The Siam Amazing Park;** which remains the oldest amusement and water park complex in Southeast Asia, a nice place for family entertainment. (nearby Suwannaphum Airport)

- Hang out and enjoy at the **Chocolate Ville** International restaurants for varieties of food (Kaset–Nawamin Road) it's not so far from Suwannaphum Airport.
- If you stay by Silom Rd. and nearby, you can enjoy a nice seafood and sea view of Bangkok **at"Talay Krungthep"**; "Talay" means "Sea", located at Bangkhuntien on Rama2 Road which is near the Gulf of Thailand.

❑ Enjoy traditional Thai Massage. There are foot massage, full massage for the whole body and massage some points like; neck and shoulder and oil massage. The massage parlours are everywhere or even by street. Say to them for "Relax" otherwise; you may get hurt after massages. Be careful!

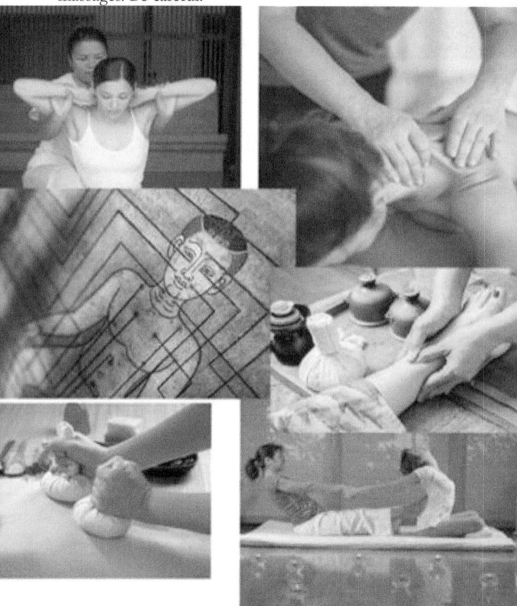

Figure 79 Thai massage

Figure 80 Muay Thai

❑ Discover **Thai Boxing or "Muay Thai",** the exciting and popular sport, from Lumpini Stadium on Raminthra Road (30 Kms. from Suwannaphum Airport) or Ratchadamnoen Stadiumon at Ratchadamnoen Road. I remembered one of my clients who loved Thai boxing and I found one camp for him to practice for about 2 weeks. He was selected to be amateur boxer in competition. He's brave and did a good job. The Thai boxing camps can be found easily nowadays. Thai Boxing is an art of fighting by using the body to be the weapon in fighting and the mind to focus where to knock down your opponent.

❑ There will be some new places coming in the future; The huge park which is honored King Bhumibol; King Rama9th, located in front of Jitlada Palace and The Marble Temple, it's built by King Rama 10th for people's park and will be finished by 2026, the land was the horse racing tracks before. The other one will be the new Zoo at Pathumthani Province and finished by 2027.

There are more attractions in Bangkok to see and to visit. I mentioned mostly the popular ones you should not miss. When you stay in Bangkok, try to walk and look around within that area.

I don't recommend you to go with taxi or tuktuk because you may waste your time with traffic and you may find some of them are not nice to you. If you join the tour or choosing the professional local guide at the beginning, you can do your own later on easily. But in case; your time is limited, I recommend the local guide for tours. My guide book is also your assistant more or less. I guarantee you enjoy Bangkok by following this guide book.

Figure 81 The Lion Guards The Marble Temple

NONTHABURI

Figure 82 the old City Hall at Nonthaburi

- ❑ Visit **Nonthaburi;** a part of Bangkok Metropolitan province which is at the northwest border of Bangkok, established since 1561. It is the most densely populated province after Bangkok. You may not know when you are in Nonthaburi!
- ❑ **Ride the Express Boat from Sathorn Pier;** major pier on the Chao Phraya River, to **Nonthaburi Pier** and to Pakkret Pier, are the most easy and fast trip. (BTS: at Saphantaksin Station for pier or MRT: Yaek Tiwanon Station and get a taxi to the pier.)
- ❑ Admire **the Former Nonthaburi Provincial Hall**, established in 1936, which is now the Nonthaburi Museum.
- ❑ Admire the Ordination Hall, Thai-Chinese architectural styles, at **Wat Chaloem Phra Kiat** on the Chao Phraya River bank opposite to Nonthaburi Pier.

❑ Exploring **Koh Kret;** the small island in the Chao Phraya River, and ride bicycle around this island where the traditional earthenware is still produced. (After visiting Nonthaburi Pier then ride a river boat to Pakkret Pier and cross the river by ferry to Koh Kret)

❑ Admire the Leaning Pagoda or "**Phra Chedi Mutao**"; a white pagoda in Burmese in Wat Paramaiyikawat on Koh Kret. It's where the Buddha's Relic was enshrined since 1884 by the King Rama V.

Figure 83 Koh Kret

❑ Discover the Big Fairs at **Impact Exhibition Center** in Nonthaburi Province areas. Check the events of the day before going there. It's a large exhibition Hall where there are many interesting events to experience, one of them is OTOP FAIR for commercial all products in Thailand with some cultural shows. (short distance from Pakkret Pier)

**At Ha Yaek Pakkret (Ha means Five, Yaek means Intersaction); 1st to the pier and local market, 2nd to Tivanon Rd. and Pathumthani, 3rd to Laksi, Bangkok, 4th to Nonthaburi town, and 5th to Wat Klang Kret opposite to Koh Kret. You can have a look at the local market here.

Figure 84 The taxi boat at Pakkret Pier

PATHUMTHANI

Figure 85 Wat Chedi Hoi

❑ **Pathumthani is another** part of Bangkok Metropolitan Region. The Province is an old city at the north of Bangkok. This province has been established since the Ayutthaya Period in the reign of King Narai. The former name was "Sam Khok" where the "Mon people" evacuated during the war. (They were minor ethnic group from Burma settled in Thailand).

Many parts of this province are hard to notice for being Bangkok or Pathumthani province.

The best way to notice Pathumthani is by riding along the Klong or Canal which are numbered; natural canals are 55 canals with the length of 180 Kms, the other 29 canals are irrigation canals. Start your ride at Rangsit District. You can go to Nakonnayok province from Rangsit by passing along these canals.

❑ **Wat Chedi Hoi** is the first attraction where most people look for in Pathumthani. It's located in Lat Lhum Kaew District. The temple was registered as a temple in 1988. Many of ancient oysters' shell from million years ago were found here and the abbot built the huge pagoda from them in 1995.

❑ Visit **Wat Sing;** the first Mon style temple, located on the west bank of the Chao Phraya River. This temple has been one of the oldest temples with old pagodas, ordination hall where they are for the Thai history research. (Travelling by Boat or car)

❑ Visit **Wat Phuet Udom at Klong 13;** known for the imaginative arts of Heaven and Hell from the Buddhist's belief about doing good will go to heaven but doing bad to hell, walk around the hall. (BTS: at Rangsit Station and continue by taxi)

❑ Admire the mural paintings depicting the story of " Tossachart Chadok" or The Buddha's ten lives at **Wat Chinwararam,** located on the west bank of The Chao Phraya River. (Travelling by Boat or car)

❑ Visit **The National Science Museum of Thailand,** the great place for enjoying and knowledge (the children love here), located at Klong 5 in Pathumthani Province. (The place is close to the airport)

- Admire **The Mon Golden Pagoda and the white jade Buddha** Statue at Wat Chedi Thong, on the west side of The Chao Phraya River in Pathumthani Province.
- Enjoy **The Dream World**, the amusement park, located in Pathum-thani Province nearby the east of Bangkok. (It's close to the airport.)
- Pathumthani is famous for noodle on the boat or we call "Kua Tiew Rue", you will see a big boat on each canal as a noodle restaurant and I never miss those whenever I reach here.

SAMUTPRAKAN

Figure 86 Phra Samut Chedi

- **When your arrive Thailand, you are entering Samut Prakan Province; or** called by Thai "Pak-nam", located at about 30 kilometers from Bangkok, where the Chao Phraya River flows into the Gulf of Thailand. It was an old town since Ayutthaya Period.

Most of tourists think they are in Bangkok City but this small town has many attractions where you can go by sky trains from Suwannaphum Airport for some sightseeing during short visit.

❏ Admire **The Giant Statue of Three-Headed Elephant Art** and see antiquities or priceless collections of Buddhist objects contained inside the statue, at **The Erawan Museum** in Samutprakan Province, located next to Bangkok's border,
   (BTS: at Chang Erawan Station)

❏ Discover the Temple of **Phra Samut Chedi;** on the island of the mouth of the Chao Phraya River, in Samut Prakan Province. (BTS: at Paknam Station exit 6 and connect the Ferry Boat at the Viboonsri Pier)

Figure 87 Three head Elephant Statue

❏ Enjoy The Crocodile Farm; it's a huge crocodile farm in Thailand where you can enjoy the exciting shows in this zoo. If you ride BTS, stop at Keha Station and get a taxi for 10 minutes.

Figure 88 Seagulls at Bang Poo at Samut Prakan

❏ Feed the flock of seagulls at Bangpoo Seaside; the nearest seaside to Bangkok, located in Samut Prakan Province. It's not so far from Suwannaphum Airport. You can try some local Thai Seafood here. The place is well known among Thai for having a Balloon Dancing Floor during weekend.

❏ The famous temple in Samut Prakan is called Wat Asokaram; it's where many Buddhists come for practicing meditation and the beautiful group of 13 Pagodas which built during the first abbot; Luang Por Lee was alive. You can walk around in the temple and to the small pier by the shore here. The mangrove forests are preserved in this temple where you can walk through the forest. The picturesque of the 13 pagoda group should be shot from the top floor of Viharn Hall during sunset.

Figure 89Wat Asokaram

- ❑ Discover **Sri Nakhon Khuean Khan Park and Botanical Garden**, Best Urban Oasis of Asia, for viewing birds and walking paths along the mangrove forest located at Saladeang District in Samutprakarn Province.
- ❑ Visit **The Ancient City;** or Ancient Siam, the museum park, dubbed as the world's largest outdoor museum. Located along the way to Bang Poo of Samut Prakan, where you can admire the replicas of the remarkable places in Thailand in this huge land.

Figure 90 The architecture in Ancient City

NAKONPATHOM

- Nakonpathom is a small province at northwest of Bangkok about 56 kilometers. This province has been known as the ancient city since Dvaravati Period (around 11th -16th century) from the archaeological evidences such as; a polished stone ax, bronze vessels like bowls, human bones, stone beads and etc.

- One day trip for Damnoensaduak Floating Market in Ratchaburi Province or a Tour to Kanchanaburi for the Bridge over the River Kwai, may add **Nakorn Pathom on the way back to Bangkok for seeing the landmark of the province which is the largest pagoda in Thailand which located at the center of town.**

- **If you drive, you can go by Phra Borom Chonnee Sky Bridge from Bangkok to Nakonpathom easily. This is not the passer by province for going to the west of the country like Kanchanaburi, but Nakonpathom has more attractions and delicious food than you expect, besides; you can enjoy riding a train and see rice fields and beautiful scenery of this town.**

- **You can** enjoy at **the Don Whai Market by the river;** for variety of local goods and food plus scenicriver trips (from rented boats). This local market area has some of the houses during King Rama VI period remains. Mostly food vendors travel by boat along **Tha Chin River.** It's at Phutthamonthon Sai 5 Lane.

- Eat **Khao Rham,** baked the sticky rice with coconut milk and nuts mixed with sugar in bamboo flasks, for snack.

PHRA PATHOM CHEDI

❑ Admire the **"Phrapathom Chedi"**; the symbol of Nakornpathom Province and one of the tallest and largest pagodas in Thailand, the name given by King Rama IV means the first holy Stupa, situated inside Wat Phra Pathom Chedi Racha Worawihan. You can ride a train at Hualumphong Railway Station or Bang Sue Grand Railway Station and buses at the Southern Bus Terminal available or get a public bus no. 84 at BTS: Punnavithi Station or Thonburi Station for Sampran District and connect the local bus to the pagoda. The other way by van to Nakonpathom Province at the Victory monument.

❑ Visit **Sanam Chandra Palace; located near the huge pagoda** in Nakornpathom. It's the former palace built by the King Rama VI, with a palace complex consists of buildings and a shrine.

❑ Walking around the areas of the Phrapathom Chedi and enjoy a local restaurant for a dish of grill pork with sweet sauce and steam rice for lunch. It's superb!

Figure 91 Sanam Chan Palace

❑ Visit **The Phuttha-Monthon**; one of the important religious site with 1000 acres built for cerebration of 2500th year of Buddhism, where the huge Buddha image in walking attitude is standing and being seen from the road. The site is surrounded by buildings, constructions from private community and companies, flower gardens and big trees. It's a popular place for exercise.

❑ Enjoy **Samphran Elephant and Cultural Show** at the Rose Garden. The Rose Garden at Suan Sampran was very famous for cultural show and elephant show in tha past. It's a place for many activities right now such as; cultural show, Thai dance, wedding party and hotel also available in the garden area near the Tha Chin River.

- ❑ Biking around **Sampran Riverside** and participate in workshop for Thai handmade products and get your handicraft back home.
- ❑ Visit the **Thai Human Imagery Museum;** the wax/fibreglass sculptures of vivid details created by the group of Thai artists, next to the Phuttha Monthon.
- ❑ Visit the **Woodland Museum;** the thousands pieces of wood carvings and wooden artwork Collections along the way to Phuttha Monthon.

Salt Field

Tha Chalom Samutsakhon

SAMUTSAKON

❑ **Samutsakon; is** a province on the southwest of Bangkok, its borders are; Samut Songkram, Ratchaburi, Nakhon Pathom and Bangkok.

This province was the trading port where Chinese junks arrived since 1548 A.D. The familiar name for Thai call this province is **"Mahachai"**. Sometimes it's not noticeable that you are in Samutsakorn or Bangkok until you see the exit sign showing the direction to Samutsakorn's downtown.

The province located at the mouth of Tha Chin River; distributed from The Chao Phraya River, flow into the sea at the Gulf of Thailand.

❑ Enjoy the seafood at the restaurant called **Krua chai Talay** near the Gulf of Thailand and get a **free boat** to see the scenery and viewing some teal birds and small freshwater duck.

❑ Discover the shrine in the middle of the sea or called **as "Phra Klang Nam"**, the **unseen of Samutsakorn Province** by a boat from Krua Chai Talay Seafood Restaurant at Phanthai Norasing Subdistrict.

❑ Take a boat for **watching the dolphins** and swarm of fish during May-October where they appear near the Gulf of Thailand.

❑ Discover the **Red Boardwalk Bridge** along the seashore surrounded by the mangrove forest during sunset.

It's known as "Dolphin Viewpoint" during November-January; when the breeze is cool.

❑ Admire **the Wooden Ordination Hall at Wat Leam Suwannaram**; the oldest temple located on The Ta Chin River bank in Samutsakorn Province.

SAMUTSONGKRAM

Figure 92 Talat Rom Hub at Samutsongkram

- **Samutsongkram; or called as "Mae Klong" by locals, is** the smallest province of Thailand with the least population. It's located next to Samutsakorn Province.
- The popular TRANSPORT is the train to Maeklong Station but if you join a tour for Damnoen Saduak Floating Market, please request for The Train Market here. It's also great for one day trip near Bangkok. The attractions people come here are for;
- Visit **Wat Petchsamut Voraviharn or "Luang Por Ban Leam Temple"**; the Buddha Statue in standing position holding the alms bowl was an old sacred Buddha for Thai Buddhists

TALAT ROM HUB

- ❑ **Discover "Talat Rom Hub"; or The Train Market** on the Mae Klong Railway Track, "Rom Hub" means "Closing Umbrella", the vendors with the tall umbrellas for preventing the sunshine and the heat, pull down their umbrellas and removed them and the goods from the tracks when the train approaches the market. They replace the goods again and open the umbrellas when the train passed.(**8 times a day; in Maeklong Station at 8.30, 11.00 , 14.30, 17.40/ out of station at 6.20, 9.00, 11.30, 15.30**)
- ❑ Visit **Amphawa Floating Market; a famous tourist attraction for local food** and enjoy a scenic view of the Mae Klong River.
- ❑ Enjoy Tha Kha Floating Market, a nice old market from Sampan Boats surrounded by coconut trees and gardens.
- ❑ Visit **Wat Chulamanee**; an ancient temple on the bank of Amphawa Canal, built in the Ayutthaya period.

Figure 93 Wat Bang Koong, Samutsongkram

Figure 94 Thaka Floating Market

☐ See an amazing ordination hall covered with the Huge Banyan Tree and the ancient Buddha Statue inside the hall at **Wat Bang Koong**.

☐ Admire the old aged Mural Paintings left faded color but showing the techniques of monochromatic painting on the four walls of the old Viharn or a ceremonial hall, depicting of Buddha's Life, which rarely found, at **Wat Bang Kapom**, 3 kilometers from downtown of Samut Songkram.

Figure 95 Samutsongkram; life style by canal

There are many resorts and hotels nearby the floating market in Samutsongkram Province. If you enjoy here, stay for drinking the atmosphere of countryside and see the local livings by the canals. Don't forget to **eat "Hoi Lort"**; a kind of mollusks found in Samutsongkram. See the nature at **Klong Khon** by speed boat and drop by Bang Khontee Floating Market.

Don't miss **The Rama II Park** for visiting the museum inside the wooden houses which were built in typical Thai styles. From Samutsongkram, you can continue to Petchaburi province and Hua Hin.

NAKONNAYOK

- ❑ Nakonnayok is the location of **Chulachomklao Royal Military Academy.**
- ❑ If you want to see an upcountry province which is convenient for traveling from Bangkok and Suwannaphum Airport, then go to Nakonnayok. You can stay at a nice resort hotel or take a one day trip. Please plan what you like to do or see. Mostly attractions are waterfalls, streams and mountains. People come here to relax because it's near Bangkok.
- ❑ Ride a train to Ong Kha Rak Station for visiting Nakornnayok. Vans are available at Rangsit or rent a car here.
- ❑ Splash the fresh water at:
- ❑ **Salika Waterfall**; in Khao Yai National Park, the big 9 tier-waterfall.

- **Klong Madue Waterfall**; for camping and admire the richness of natural forests and waterfall with nature surroundings.
- Swim in the big natural pool of **Nang Rong Waterfall**; it's a medium size waterfall, 20 kilometers from town. There are resorts and hotels with facilities.

Figure 96 Wang Ta Krai, Nakonnayok

Figure 97 Salika Waterfall

❑ **White-Water-Rafting in Wang Ta Krai** during July – October is the good time to enjoy and relax.

❑ White-Water-Rafting at **Kaeng Sam Chan** (means The three-storey rapids) good for swimming and rafting or adventurous tour here.

- Explore **Khun Dan Prakarn Chon Dam**; the longest roller compacted concrete Dam in the world; 2720 meter long, 93 meter high, initiated project from His Majesty The King Bhumipol or King Rama 9th ; which aimed for helping people in agriculture and preventing the flood. The dam was completed in 2005. There are fascinating scenery around the dam.
- Canoeing in **Huay Plue Water Reservoir;** the Center of Water Sport in Nakonnayok. Enjoy the picturesque of the misty morning here.
- **Adventure the jungle near Khao Yai by** hiring the boat across the lake in the dam and trek until the waterfall in the jungle, refreshing by swimming in the cool water. The boat trip cost between 1000-1500 Bahts.
- Discover **The Khun Dan Prakan Chon DamMuseum; it's the place where** telling about Nakornnayok History and the dam's construction.

- ❑ Experience overnight trekking trip around the foothills of Khao Yai National Park. It starts from Sarika waterfall and Nang Rong waterfall. Booking advance at Khao Yai National Park Office is necessary.
- ❑ **Golfing** at The Royal Hills Golf Club; a very beautiful championship standard golf course at the foothills of Khao Yai, many facilities available here and it's about 14 kilometers from town.
- ❑ **Fun drives ATVs** (All Terrain Vehicles) around the dirt track circuits.
- ❑ Kayaking and camping at **Wang Bon Water Reservoir**, the heaven of campers.
- ❑ Enjoy the local market at Luang Por Pak Daeng Temple.
- ❑ Climb the top of **Nang Buat Hill**; where situated the Replica of Buddha's Footprint. Many worshippers like to place some gold leaves on; for good luck, and enjoy the nice view of Nakornnayok countryside on the hilltop.
- ❑ Visit **Chulachomklao Royal Military Academy**; a Thai cadet school with large areas which also full of attractions. You need the car or bicycle for moving around for seeing:
- ❑ See the 100 Year Royal Military Academy Museum
- ❑ See the King Rama V Monument
- ❑ See Khun Dan Shrine, the war hero.
- ❑ See the Golf Course
- ❑ Try some activities like; parachute drill by jumping down a cable slide, sports in stadium and 25 meter long swimming pool.

Figure 98 Maha Pucha Buddhist Memorial at Nakonnayok

❑ Visit the areas of **Maha Pucha Buddhist Memorial**; the temple of displaying the important event when The Buddha (represented by the huge sitting Buddha image) and His 1,250 Disciples (the small statues placed in front of the Buddha) assembled together without making any appointments on Full Moon of the 3ʳᵈ Month of Buddhist Calendar.

It's the day Lord Buddha presented Patimok Teaching or the monk's mission in this meeting and it's called "Makha Pucha Day". The memorial is located near Salika Waterfall.

❑ See the lake full of red lotus near by the highway; to Ban Na District.

- ❏ Visit **Wat Maneewong** in town; admire the beautiful cave decorated with naka. (the sacred serpents from the legend of Buddha's History)
- ❏ Admire the big pavilion built in Khmer architecture at **Wat Khiriwan**, about 9 kilometers from downtown.
- ❏ See the rice fields at Phu Kalieng; where there is wooden bridge for walking in the field.
- ❏ Admire the natural bamboo tunnel in front of **Wat Chulapornvanaram** in Ban Na District; one of a popular shot of Nakornnayok.
- ❏ Drop by Home Flower Garden Village at Klong 15, in Ongkarak District near Bangkok.

Figure 99 Khun dan Prakan Chon Dam

SUPHANBURI

Figure 100 Wat Phai Rong Wua at Suphanburi

❑ Suphanburi is one of the ancient cities which located at the northwest of Bangkok about 107 kms. It was the site of many wars with Burmese. It's quiet close to Nakonpathom and Kanchanaburi. Travel by car takes about an hour; much easier, by passing through Nonthaburi.

You can ride a train for Suphanburi Station. It's a nice town for one day sight seeing and become one of the popular provinces for tourists during weekend.

❑ Visit **Wat Pa Lei Lai**; the old temple located at the center of town, where the sacred huge sitting Buddha Statue is well known among Thai "Luang Por Tho" situated. The height is 23 meter.

❑ Visit **Don Chedi Monument**; the commemoration of King Naresuan The Great; of his Victory in the Elephant Battle against King Maha Upparacha of Burma in 1592.

Figure 101 Don Chedi, Suphanburi

❑ Walk around at **Wat Phai Rong Wua; an amazing temple with** many images represents Hell and Heaven displayed.

• The biggest Buddha image sitting outdoor is called **Phra Kakusantho.**

- The bronze Buddha Statue is called **"Phra Buddha Khodom"**; with the height of 26 meters and 10 meter-wide. This Buddha image was built in 1959 and took 17 years for constructing. This is the biggest bronze Buddha statue in Thailand.
- ❑ Walk around the old market of Suphanburi at **Talat Bang Li**; where the old style of living remained and many nice food to try here; like, boiled Duck with black bean sauce, river fish menu, Sali Cake, etc.
- ❑ Admire the beautiful huge Buddha Statue carved on the **Mangkorn Bin Cliff** near the hill in U-Thong district area. The outstanding image is 108 meter high and 88 meter wide.

Figure 102 Mankorn Bin Cliff, Suphanburi

Figure 103 Dragon at the city pillar shrine, Suphanburi

- ❑ Admire the unique shape of big dragon sculpture at the Museum of the Descendants of Dragon or Heaven Dragon Park; which established to celebrate 20 years of Thailand – China Diplomatic relationship in 1996.
- ❑ See The City Pillar Shrine near the Dragon Museum.
- ❑ Explore **"The 100 year Market"** by Tha Chin River **at Sam Chuk District;** this market received an Award of Merit in 2009; the annual UNESCO Asia-Pacific Heritage Awards for Culture Heritage Conservation, there are many two-storey wooden buildings and houses of the old days still remain original Thai style. The small lanes of the market are full of street food and various kinds of goods.
- ❑ Don't forget to visit Bueng Chawak Chalermphrakiat; a fresh water lake and a large aquarium with many kinds of water animals. The place is nice and interesting.

AYUTTHAYA

Figure 104 Wat Yai Chai Mongkon, Ayutthaya

AYUTTHAYA

❑ Ayutthaya was the former capital city for 417 years before it's destroyed by the Burmese Army in 1767; the official name is called **"Phra Nakorn Si Ayutthaya"**.

The province is about 75 kilometers from Bangkok. The trip for Ayutthaya; can do for one day tour by road and by river cruise. If you would like to relax and see more details than the package tour, you may have to stay in Ayutthaya Town and explore by yourself. There are TukTuk vehicles for taking you anywhere you want. It's an amazing city and attracts anyone who enters the town; by the ruined, old style houses, river view, food and all the temples around the town. I usually choose to go to Ayutthaya during weekend. I have a one day trip to show for example; in case you don't have much time.

The ruins of the old capital have been a UNESCO World Heritage Site; located in the heart of the city, which is called **"The Ayutthaya Historical Park"**.

TRANSPORT TO AYUTTHAYA:

❑ **RAIL:** Trains for Ayutthaya Railway Station is in town, Ban Phachi Junction and Bang Pa-In Railway Station which is close to Bang Pa-In Palace.

❑ **ROAD:** Buses at the Northern Bus Terminal.

❑ **BOAT: Express boats.**

Figure 105 Chedi Wat Sam Pluem, Ayutthaya

ONE DAY TRIP IN AYUTTHAYA

One day trip in Ayutthaya should be started early in the morning; if you leave Bangkok about 7 am, you should arrive by 9 am. When entering in Ayutthaya, what you will see;

❑ **See the Chedi Wat Sam Pluem**; a pagoda situated in the middle of the circle of main road during entering Ayutthaya Town. This pagoda was assumed to be built before the Fall of Ayutthaya.

❑ **Wat Yai Chaimongkol** was an old temple built since the beginning of Ayutthaya Period. This beautiful temple is the first temple you meet when you enter Ayutthaya Town, after passing the old pagoda in the circle.

❑ Climb up the top of the historic huge Pagoda inside Wat Yai Chai Mongkon. It's the tallest pagoda in Ayutthaya and the memorial for the Victory of King Naresuan the Great.

Walk around the pagoda and enjoy the scenery of the Historical Park from the highest viewpoint.

Admire the beautiful image of Buddha Statue inside The Ordination Hall of Wat Yai Chaimongkon.

❑ Admire the old Reclining Buddha outdoor because the building is left ruined; only the brick walls and some columns remain for the shape of the hall. The Buddha is near the entrance of Wat Yai Chaimongkol.

❑ **Admire Luang Por Tho at Wat Phanan Choeng;** the statue is the biggest Buddha Statue in Ayutthaya, with the width of 14.20 meters and the height is 19.20 meters, made of stucco cladded with gold sheets. This sitting position Buddha image is in the attitude of calling the earth to witness or Maravijaya attitude.

Figure 106 Luang Por Tho Wat Phanan Choeng

❑ **Wat Phanan Choeng;** one of the oldest temples in Ayutthaya, the historical background has been unknown, assumed; it's the temple before Ayutthaya was the capital. The temple is located on the east bank of The Chao Phraya River. The famous Buddha statue which is called "Luang Por Sum Por Khong" (Chinese Name) or "Luang Por Tho" is the biggest Buddha image in Ayutthsya.

• Admire the Golden Buddha statue; made of pure gold with 1.5 meters wide and 2 meters high in the hall of "Luang Por Tho".

❏ See **Chao Mae Soi Dok Mak Shrine;** a memorial of love story between a Thai king of Ayutthaya and the Chinese Princess. The shrine is the mixed art of Thai and Chinese style.

Figure 107 The ruined pagoda at Wat Phra sisanpeth and wat Monkonborpit nearby.

Brief history of Ayutthaya:

When you reach Wat Monkonborpit, you will arrive at the ruined palace and the temples within the historical park areas. Sometimes people choose to come here at the beginning and then see Wat Phananchoeng and Wat Yai Chai Monkon later.

The Ayutthaya City was found in 1351 by King Rama Thibodi; the first king of Ayutthaya Kingdom (1350-1369) who was known as King U-Thong. (The statue of the king is situated in U-Thong District, Suphanburi Province.

Ayutthaya was destroyed by Burmese Army in 1767 and lost many valuable and artistic objects. It was the capital for 417 years and after that, Thonburi was the capital and then Bangkok.

❑ The Historical Park was announced as the national archaeological Site in 1976 and the Fine Arts Department of Thailand renovated the ruins and specified the lists within the park; The Royal Palace, Wat Mahathart, Wat Phra Si Sanphet, Wat Ratchaburana, Wat Phra Ram and The Viharn of Wat Monkon Borpit. In 1997; the areas cover 22 places were added in the lists of the park site.

❑ **The part of this park was declared a UNESCO World Heritage Site in 1991.**

THE AYUTTHAYA HISTORIC PARK

Figure 108 The sign of Moradok Lok or a cultural world heritage by Unesco, the ruined palace and temple, Ayutthaya

❑ Explore **The Ayutthaya Historic Park** and enjoy walking around the ruined palace and temples. There are boards for historical background of each area includes signs for directions in the park. Normally we start from the Viharn of Wat Monkon Borpit where the palace and temples are around this area:

Figure 109 Wat Phra sisanpeth, Ayutthaya

- ❖ **The Old Palace** was established in 1350. It was destroyed during the war with The Burmese Army and it's the end of the Ayutthaya Period since that time.

- ❖ **Wat Phra Sri Sanpetch** was established in 1448. This temple was in the area of the Old Palace. It's the model of Wat Phra Keaw or the Temple of The Emerald Buddha at The Grand Palace.

- ❖ **Wat Mahathat** was established to be the monastery in 1374. The famous photo of "The Face of Buddha Image" inserted in the hollow at the base of a large tree is here. The Buddha's head is made of sand stone; it's assumed that the Buddha's head was broken during renovating and fell to the ground of Bho Tree about 50 years ago, after that the tree's roots cover the head and become the famous unseen Thailand to the world. The photo was one of the selected photos by Unesco from all the world heritages. The temple also found with a very beautiful pagoda built in octagon shape.

❖ **Wat Ratchaburana**; was established in D. 1424, one of the oldest and largest monastery during Ayutthaya Period, known as "The Treasure Trove of Ayutthaya" found at the temple's crypt at the main shrine or "Phra Prang" inside the temple.

Figure 110 Wat Ratchaburana, Ayutthaya

- ❖ **Wat Phra Ram;** was established in 1369, located opposite to Wat Mongkon Borpit, in front of a lake called as "Bueng Phra Ram"; "Bueng" means lake or lagoon, contains of 7 buildings and the big shrine or "Phra Prang" which left ruined. The beautiful interior of this Khmer Prang Shrine are the mural paintings on the wall.

- ❖ **Wat Monkolborpit;** a temple is assumed to be built in 1448-1488 in the reign of Phra Borom Matrai Lokkanat, the eight king of Ayutthaya Kingdom. The temple was renovated many times until 1956, the building and the Buddha image was renovated as seen nowadays.

Figure 111 Wat Monkon Borpit, Ayutthaya

❖ The beautiful hall is a hall of Phra Monkon Borpit; which is the huge Buddha Statue made of bronze and lacquer gilded, has been assumed that the statue was built at the beginning of Ayutthaya Period with the size of 9.55 meters wide and 12.45 meters high. The statue was put outdoor before and restored many times.

❖ After the site was declared a UNESCO World Heritage in 1991, The Fine Arts Department of Thailand renovated the ruins and this national historical park covers more areas.

*For one day trip of Ayutthaya town were mainly mentioned from the beginning till here in town and may include **Bang Pa In Palace** as well.

Figure 112 Bang Pa-In, Ayutthaya

BANGPA IN

❑ **Bang Pa In Palace was an old palace built in 1630-1656 during Phra Chao Prasat Thong reigned; 24th king of Ayutthaya Kingdom. The palace built for a temporary overnight stay for the kings during travelling in this areas.**

❑ After 2nd fall of Ayutthaya; 1765-1767, the palace was left abandoned, King Rama V renovated, rebuilt and added more buildings inside the palace for making it a royal guest house and a banquet palace.

The palace is about 18 kilometers from downtown. Ride the train from Bangkok and stop at Bang Pa In Station.

❑ Discover **Wat Niwate Thammaprawat;** opposite to The Bang Pa-In Palace, an amazing architectural style of Gothic Revival for Buddhist Temple. The hall was built in the reign of King Rama V in 1878 and served as a royal temple. This beautiful hall is decorated with stained glass windows and a Gothic altar for Buddha image. The temple received the ASA Architectural Conservation Award in 1989.

❑ The Department of Fine Art in Thailand declared more places to be national archaeological sites within Ayutthaya areas; after Ayutthaya was praised as a cultural world heritage by UNESCO, by renovating and developing in order to preserve the old capital city to be more interesting. If you stay few days in Ayutthaya, you can roam around the city for more places, I would like to give the lists for you to explore more when you have more days here.

❑ Chantara Kasem Palace
❑ Wat Suwandararam Ratworaviharn
❑ Wat Lokhaya Sutharam
❑ Wat Thamikarat
❑ Wat Senasnaram Ratworaviharn
❑ Wat Suan Luang Sop Sawan
❑ City walls and Fortifications
❑ Wat Chaiwattanaram
❑ Wat Putthaisawan
❑ Wat Na Phramain
❑ Wat Kasatti Ratworaviharn
❑ Wat Kudi dao
❑ Wat Dusitaram
❑ Wat Phu Khao Thong
❑ Wat Phraya Man
❑ Portugal Village

- ❑ Holland Village
- ❑ Japanese Village
- ❑ Paniet Klonk Chang
- ❑ The Cathedral of Saint Joseph ETC.

- ❖ **Wat Chaiwatthanaram**; the beauty of this monastery can be seen at the west bank of The Chao Phraya River outside the city. It's built in Khmer or Cambodian architecture like, "Angkor Wat" style.

- ❖ **Wat Kudi Dao**, the late Ayutthaya architecture, has been the legend for Thai talk of "The Hidden Treasure" possessed by the spirits of the owners from Ayutthaya Period.

- ❖ **Phra Chedi Suriyothai,** the memorial of The Brave Queen Suriyothai who joined the war with the Burmese Army by riding on the elephant and was killed.

Figure 113 Wat Chiwattanaram, Wat Kudi Dao, Wat Phukhaothong, Ayutthaya

❖ **Japanese Village.**

❖ Must visit the **Sam Phraya Museum** for admiring many ancient items and some treasures found from the ruined monastries.

❖ **Wat Phu Khao Thong**; the huge pagoda, built in mixed Thai and Burmese architecture with 90 meters high, located about 2 kilometers away from town.

❖ **The Elephant Kraal Pavilion or Paniet Klonk Chang,** the place where the elephants were round up in front of the royal family.

ANGTHONG

Figure 114 Luang Por Yai at Wat Muang, Angthong

Angthong is a little town next to Ayutthaya, located on The Chao Phraya River bank, known as "Wiset Chaichan Town". It was the frontier outpost of Ayutthaya during the war with Burmese Army. The population here is approximately 14,000 only.

❏ Admire the huge Reclining Buddha Statue; the length is 50 meters, the 2nd largest in Thailand located at Wat Inthapramoon; the old temple since Sukhothai Period. (the largest is at Wat Bang Plee yai in Samutprakarn)

Figure 115Court Dolls, Angthong

- ❑ Visit **Bangsadet; the Court Doll Center** which established by Her Majesty The Queen Sirikit of King Rama 9, to be the center of villagers' craftsmanship and become one of their earnings from these art works to visitors. You can watch the demonstration of making dolls from clay; sold for only 15 Bahts a piece only. The location is in Wat Sutthawat.

- ❑ Discover the old ordination hall covered with Pho Trees around; believed that the hall was built about 400 years ago, having the Buddha Statue in the hall at **Wat Sang Kha Tai, one of the Unseen Thailand.**

- ❑ Visit **Wat Chaiyo**; the popular temple among Thai Buddhists, come for paying respect to The Sacred Big Buddha Statue; called as " Luang Por Tho" and walk around the temple and have a nice view nearby the river.

❏ Admire the other old Reclining Buddha of **Wat Pamok**; the oldest temple since Sukhothai Period.

❏ Discover the **Aekarat Village**; where the famous place for Thai drum-making, the best handicraft and most well known in Thailand. It was established since 1827. You can watch the drum-making process and get the small Thai drum as a souvenir.

❏ Admire the largest Sitting Buddha Image in the world; called **"Luang Por Yai",** at Wat Moung in Wiset Chai Chan District. The height is 95 meters; a place where we can only pay respect to The Buddha's finger nail only.

LOPBURI

Figure 116 Phra Prang Samyod

❑ **Lopburi** Province is known as the Kingdom of Somdej Phra Narai; who was one of the Great King of Siam during Ayutthaya Period. It's only 150 kilometers from Bangkok, next to Ayutthaya Province and the route is heading to the north of Thailand. You can stay here few days for exploring this old province.

Figure 117 Wang Narai, Lopburi

❑ This province was called "La Woa"; which comes from the Khmer or Cambodian architecture; which is found at **The Phra Prang Sam Yod** situated in the center of town, many artifacts, historical structures and prehistoric settlements discovered in this old town.

❑ King Narai, the Great, made this city as the second capital; for, Ayutthaya was threatened by the Dutch at that time. When the king died, his palace was abandoned until King Rama IV came in Lopburi and renovated the old palace in 1856.

Transportation:
Rail: Stop at Lopburi Station, walk to Phra Prang Sam yod and you can look around the downtown conveniently.

Bus: Get the bus at Northern Bus Terminal near Jatujak Park.

Van: Get the van from the Van-Point opposite to Future Park Rangsit Community Mall. This is an easy way for fast travelling.

Car/Taxi: Ride north route and see the exit sign.

❏ Admire **Phra Prang Sam Yod**; the landmark of

Lopburi, declared as the museum of national heritage situated near the railway station (about 200 meters). This Khmer style architectural three Towers; called "Prang", made of brick and stucco; the north tower dedicated to Prajnaparamita (the Perfection of Wisdom), the central to the Buddha and the other to Avalokitasvara who embodies the compassion of all Buddhas. It was assumed to be built since 1191-1224.

There are a large number of monkeys around Lopburi Town especially at San Phra Kan; Lopburi's Sacred Shrine from long time ago. The shrine seems to be the resident of monkey populations. Please be careful because many of them are not friendly; but if you just ignore them, they won't disturb you.

❑ There is a famous annual festival for Monkey Buffet at San Phra Kan, Phra Prang Sam Yod and nearby the market areas which are a big event in Lopburi Town and attract all tourists for looking at monkeys enjoy eating plenty of fruits and desserts.

❑ See the Statue of **King Narai the Great;** this is to honor the king from bringing prosperity and peace to this town in his period. If you come by road, you will see the statue when you enter the Lopburi Town.

❑ Visit **Wat Phra Sri Mahathat;** the ancient temple with a very beautiful, biggest Prang.

Figure 118 Wat Phra Sri Mahathat, Lopburi

Figure 119 Wang Narai; the satatue of King Narai the Great with offering from worshippers who visit Wang Narai

Figure 120 Train for sight seeing at Pasak Dam

- ❑ Explore The **Pasak Chonlasit Dam;** The Royal Project of His Majesty King Bhumipol or King Rama 9th . This is the Research and Development dam and Reservoir; for agriculture, industries and preventing from flood. It's the largest reservoir in Central Thailand, located about 60 kilometers from town.

- ❑ Enjoy riding the tourist-train across The Pasak Chonlasit Dam during November-January (available7.30am-6.30pm) for admiring picturesque scenery of surroundings and drinking fresh air.

- ❑ Refresh with the fascinating sunflower fields. Lopburi is known as Thailand's largest sunflower plantation; full blooming seen in November to January on the way to **Pattana Nikom District.**

- ❑ Drop by **Wat Khao Chin Lae;** a beautiful temple near a hill, you can climb up the hill along stairs of 439 steps.

- ❏ Admire the historical landmark of **Tha Hin at Ban Chao Wichayen**; the Royal Reception House in the reign of King Narai, it's left ruined but still maintained well.

- ❏ Explore the compound of **Narai Ratchaniwet Palace or "Wang Narai" which was built in 1666. The** palace was for the king's resident and a royal guest house. It's also King Narai's last palace and was abandoned after the king died in 1688.

  The palace was restored by the order of King Rama IV and more of buildings constructed within the compound in 1856.

  The areas of the Palace become The National Heritage called "Som Dej Phra Narai National Museum" for old items exhibition.

  The Palace are divided into 3 parts; the Outer, the Central and the Inner Walls.

- ❏ Discover the viewpoint of Lopburi at **Khao Phraya Doen Thong**. It'a about 4 kms. to go up from the ground along steep pathway up to the hill for a fantastic view. You can use the bicycle or pickup truck to reach the peak of the hill but the road is not so good.

- ❏ Discover nice fresh and clear water of Kan **Lueng Waterfall**; in Chai Badan National Park.

- ❏ Explore the **Lung of Lopburi at Sap Lek Water Reservoir**; built in the reign of King Narai the Great. It was a water-supply for the palace. This Water Reservoir is surrounded by mountains and forests where public now go for relaxation.

- ❏ Admire the amazing Entrance of **Wat Koong Ta Lao in Ban Mee District.** It's built in Hanuman Figure opens his mouth; it's the Monkey Character from The Ramayana Epic.

Figure 121Wat Koong Ta Lao, Lopburi

❑ Going up the hilltop by stairs of 3,790 steps to admire The Buddha's Relic Pavilion at **Wat Khao Wong Phra Chan**; the highest hill of Lopburi. "Phra Chan" means "Moon". There is a festival of "Faith" which is a tradition for worshipping the Buddha, started during Chinese New Year Festival; the worshippers will climb the staircases to the top for worshipping to the Buddha's Footprint on the highest hill here. It's also for admiring a beautiful moon shines all over the mountain and the big Buddha image there. The temple will be opened during this traditional worshipping 24 hours for 15 days once a year only. I climbed to the top of the mountain during the day time long time ago, I enjoyed the views there but the weather was so hot that time.

❑ Visit **Wat Khao Phra Ngam**; a beautiful temple nearby downtown, where the huge statue of Buddha Image built on the hill. It's unknown for the temple's historical background.

Figure 122 Khao Wong Phra Chan, Lopburi

Most of the places in Thailand like subdistricts, districts and hills had the legends behind their names. One of the legends was the love story of Khao Wong Phra Chan; a story of Nang Nong Pra Chan, her lover and a Chinese merchant. It happened when the Chinese merchant wanted to marry Nong Pra Chan but her lover broke the wedding plan. They all were dead from fighting and finally many places were named from the legend included her name became "Wong Phra Chan" and many names of hills around here came from the old legend. Some people said that; to climb up the top of Khao Wong Phra Chan was an effort by using "Heart and Love" in stead of using "Strength". I hope you will do it once!

Figure 123 Wat Phra Phutthabat at Saraburi; The Buddha's Footprint inside Phra Mondop

SARABURI

❑ Saraburi is a province on the way to the northeast of Thailand. It's where most Thai Buddhists stop at Wat Phra Phutthabat; for paying respects to the sacred Buddha's Footprint; which is known for nationwide as the landmark of Saraburi. The Footprint is covered with a beautiful Mondop building on a hill. Mondop is a square building with spire-roof and decorations.

This province locates in the central part of Thailand and about 100 kms from Bangkok. It's assumed that the province was established in 1549

- You can experience riding a train to Saraburi Station or Kaeng Khoi Junction.
- **Wat Phra Phutthabat**; or "The Temple of Buddha's Footprint", believed by the worshippers that The Buddha left here and people come for putting the gold leaves on the Footprint. There is Tradition for worshipping the Buddha's Footprint Festivals held twice a year in February and March. The size of this footprint is 21 inches wide and 5 feet long.
- Visit **Wat Phra Phutthachai**; the temple where it's believed that there's the shadow of Buddha in standing position seen on the cliff of the hill. This temple is located in town.
- Splash and swim in clear water during November-April at **Chet Sau Noi Waterfall** National Park in Muak Lek District. The waterfall is 7 tier waterfalls with a wide basin, popular for swimming.

Figure 124 NamTok Chet Sao Noi, Saraburi

SINGBURI

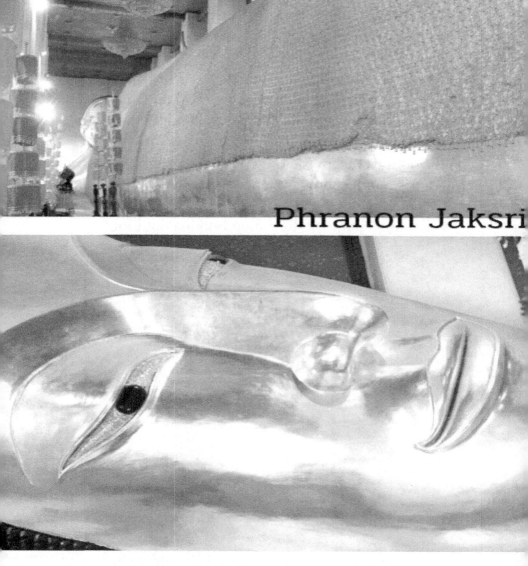

Phranon Jaksri

Figure 125 Phra NonJaksri, Singburi

❑ Singburi Province is about 142 kms to the north of Bangkok. It's established in 1895 during King Rama V period, from the consolidation of 3 small towns (Sing Buri, In Buri and Phrom Buri) on the bank of Chao Phraya River.

- Most tourists enjoy **Singburi Fish Eating Festival.** It's a natural fresh water catfish is known for Thai as "Mae La" found plenty of them here. The popular recipes are grilled or deep fried with herbal plants served with spicy sauce.

❏ The large Reclining Buddha at **Wat Phra Non Jaksri** is the landmark of Singburi, travel about 3 kilometers from downtown. The statue was built in beautiful Sukhothai Style with 46 meter- long.

❏ If you travel from the north back to Bangkok, you will see a beautiful temple named Wat Phra Prang Munee in Singburi. It's a beautiful temple with Prang Pagoda and a huge statue of Reclining Buddha outdoor.

Figure 126Wat Phra Prang Munee at Singburi

CHAINAT

❑ Chainat is a province on the way to the north of Thailand. It's about 200 kms from Bangkok. The name of the province means "Place of Victory" because the Burmese Army were defeated in Chainat every time the battle happened in the past.

Chainat is a quiet and peaceful town. You may stop a while during the journey to the north for enjoy some sight-seeing here. The famous attractions are Bird Park and the dam here.

❑ Explore **Chainat Bird Park;** the largest bird park in Thailand and the largest aviary in Asia. There are more than 100 species of the birds; the releasing ones in nature, with some in the cages, and the park also has fresh water fish aquarium.

❑ Visit **The Chao Phraya Dam;** a barrage dam built at the bend of the Bang Krabien River in 1957, which regulates the flow of The Chao Phraya River into the lower central Thailand to 17 provinces. The best time for a nice view is in January and February.

❑ Experience wildlife at Wasan Crocodile Farm near the dam.

❑ **Wat Thammamoon Voraviharn,** the Temple of Chainat Kingdom in the past. It locates near the hill, with an old beautiful bronze Standing Buddha Statue. It's about 8 kilometers from town.

❑ **Wat Prathommatesana Aranyawasri** or Wat Khao Plong; the hillside temple with a stunning Buddha Statue. It's the best viewpoint for Chainat Province.

❑ There are many beautiful temples in Chainat; such as, Wat Pak Klong Makhamtao, Wat Karuna, Wat Phra Kaew, Wat Mahathart and Wat Phra Borommathat Woraviharn for visiting and taking photos.

UTHAITHANI

Figure 127 Offering to a monk on Sakae Krang River, Uthaithani

❑   Uthaithani is a small town which known for Thung Yai Huay Kha Kheang; the wildlife sanctuary, a UNESCO Natural World Heritage site. If you would like to see rural area which still has a touch of old days, you should not miss Uthaithani.

❑ It's about 210 kilometers from Bangkok to the north. When I entered the town late in the afternoon, I found that the town was so quiet. I heard that many tourists here during weekend only.

❑ Stay in downtown is more convenient for walking around this peaceful town and see the local Thai livings along the Sakae Krang River.

❑ Morning walk in town and see a beautiful sunrise at **The Morning Market** nearby Sa Kae Krang River; the main river of Uthaithani.

Figure 128 The Morning Market, Uthaithani

❑ Take a look at the big communities of local people living in raft houses near the market opposite to Wat Osatharam; an old temple of this town. It's a peaceful and simple life here.

Figure 129 Wat Osatharam, Uthaithani

❏ Admire the ordination hall of **Wat Osatharam**; the old temple since Ayutthaya period, locates at the other side of the river.

❏ Walk along the river bank in the early morning and across at the bridge nearby the market to the temple.
Enjoy a boat trip along Sa Kae Krang River to admire the local raft-livings.

❏ Taste a local coconut ice cream and some custard bread; the signature snack from Uthaithani, at a small wooden shop of old style in town.

❏ Enjoy eating local Thai food and desserts with lots of entertainments at the Walking Street at Trok Rong Ya; Trok means lane, on Saturday only.
This walking street is for tourist entertainment and makes Uthaithani busy during weekend.

WAT THA SOONG

Figure 130Luang Por Ruesi Lingdum, Wat Thasoong, Uthaithani

- ❑ **Wat Tha Soong** or Wat Jantharam is the main destination for mostly tourists. It's a famous temple among Thai Buddhists worshippers of Luang Por Lue Sri Ling Dum; the well-known monk who was the former abbot here. There are many beautiful buildings built when he was alive; such as, Viharn Kaew, the ordination hall, Maha Viharn and Kings Memorials.
- ❑ Discover stunning landscape at **Ban Chai Khao or Thai- Switzerland** in Lan Sak District.
- ❑ Explore **Hup Pa Tat;** a tunnel through limestone cliffs to see a unique rainforests.

This amazing forest is very humid, full of "Tat Tree" and natural rare plants. It was discovered in 1979 by a monk and become a preservation of wildlife in Thailand in 1984.

❑ Trail to Hup Pa Tat along 700 meter long nature trails for about half an hour, pass through a dark cave to the large chimney where the light shines on Tat Forests. It looks like in the prehistoric forests surrounded by natural rare plants and limestone hills.

❑ Adventure into The Wildlife Sanctuary at Huai Kha Kheang National Park at Lansak District, away from Uthaithani downtown about 100 kilometers.It's a large wildlife sanctuary in Thailand and connects to Thung Yai Naresuan Wildlife Sanctuary (in Kanchanaburi and Tak); the two sanctuaries occupy about 622,000 hectares contained of large animals and one of the richest forests in Southeast Asia. They are registered as a natural world heritage by UNESCO in 1991.

❑ Huai Kha Khaeng Wildlife Sanctuary is a natural wonder for photographer- adventurers who camp for shooting pictures of"Big 7"; elephants, Indochinese tigers, leopard, wild water buffalo, Banteng (kind of cattle), gaur and tapir.

The popular time for visiting the sanctuary and camping is during the dry season. Please contact the Conservation Office in Bangkok or at Huai Kha Khaeng Office.

One of the well known festivals in Uthaithani is "Tak Bat Thewo Festival" at Wat Sankas Rattana Khiri.

It's a tradition performed the day after the end of Buddhist Lent Day; by offering food to monks who walk from the top of the hill to the ground for the alms.

This is an event to remind of Lord Buddha (from the Pali Buddhist Canon, collection of scriptures in Theravada Buddhist tradition) when he came from Daovadueng Heaven after Preaching Dhamma(His Teaching) to his mother. This event is worth to see.

Here I was at the hill foot of Sakae Krang Hill of Wat Sangkas Rattana Khiri; a beautiful temple in Uthaithani Town, where you can climb 499 steps to the Viharn Hall. It's the place where the sacred Buddha Statue situated; the Buddha's Relic kept inside the head part of the statue. Have a nice view on the hilltop.

Figure 131 Wat Sangkas Rattana Khiri, Uthaithani

NAKON SAWAN

- ❏ Nakon Sawan is "The Gate to The North". It's wide known for Chinese New Year Celebration Day; a great New Year Festival celebrated for more than 100 years continuously by Thai-Chinese of this province.
- ❏ Nakon Sawan has been called as "Pak Nam Pho" since Ayutthaya period. It's the province where Ping, Wang, Yom and Nan Rivers joined together and become the main river; The Chao Phraya River's origin.
- ❏ It's about about 250 kilometers from Bangkok and locates about half way to go to Chiang Mai. It's also a junction for rails and buses to other provinces.

There are many hotels in downtown for the travellers and various kinds of delicious food which are the main attractions for tourists who mostly stop a night. The tourist attractions normally choose to visit the landmark for Nakon Sawan which is Khao Kop or the temple Wat Khao Kop, Khao Nor and Bueng Bora Petch.

Figure 132 Bueng Bora Petch

❑ Ride a boat and admire many things within the areas of **Bueng Bora Petch**; the largest lake in Thailand covers 224 km^2, with more than 140 species of water animals; like, fresh water fish, crocodiles, birds and etc.

❏ In the boat trip; you pass by many important places, such as; The Inland Fisheries Research and Development Regional Center, Phra Thamnak Plae Summer Palace, many lotus flowers in the lake. Discover **Nakhon Sawan Tower** in town where you can see the areas of Nakhon Sawan on the ninth floor.

❏ Visit **Wat Khiri Wong;** one of the important temples with the outstanding pagoda on the hilltop, seen from far distance, it's one of a good viewpoints.

❏ Admire the beautiful Bhoghaya Pagoda at **Wat Pa Siri Rattana Visuth. The pagoda is** modeled from the famous Bhuddha Gaya Pagoda in India.

❏ Visit **San Chao Mae Tabtim;** the Chinese sacred Shrine for Thai-Chinese, where The Grand Chinese New Year Festival performs.

❏ Discover **Pasan;** the new look landmark of Nakhon Sawan, built in modern style of buildings which looks alike 2 rivers meet together. There are some exhibitions of Nakhon Sawan history inside these buildings.

❏ Visit **Khao Kop** and Wat Woranat Bunpot; an old temple at Khao Kop. The height of this hill is about 185 meters; you can go by car or walk on 437 steps of the staircase to reach the top for panorama view of Nakonsawan province. There are a golden pagoda, replica of Buddha's footprint and Buddha Statue on the hilltop of the temple.

❏ **Going up the vertical staircase at Khao Nor;** the lime stone hills where the trails are mostly steep steps to the top. You have to be careful of monkeys around here. The hill can be seen along the highway outside town. **You need to be healthy and strong for this challenge.** It's very steep and slippery staircase before reaching the top of the hill.

The height of the hill is 680 steps along the cement stairs trail and the rest are very steep (almost straight line) for hiking up to the top of the hill.

The hilltop is for a scenic landscape of Nakon Sawan; seeing like, paddy fields and some of agricultural areas as far as the eyes can see. Absolutely worth the tiredness that has come up!!

Figure 133 Khao Nor

KAM PHAENG PHET

Figure 134 Temple in Kam Phaeng Phet Historical Park

❑ Explore Kam Phaeng Phet by going to **The Kam Phaeng Phet Historical Park which** locates at the east of the bank of Ping River in town. It's on the way to the upper north of Thailand. If you travel by road, the vendors for handicrafts and small bananas seen from the sides of the highway.

When you have a package tour of Sukhothai, Kam Phaeng Phet will be added for its historical park.

This historical park is a part of Historic Town of **Sukhothai and Associated Historic Towns** which is the UNESCO Cultural World Heritage Sites. These Sites consist of Sukhothai Historical Park, Srisatchanalai Historical Park and Kam Phaeng Phet Historical Park. The structures and town plan are quiet similar to Sukhothai's.

The large sculptures and architectures within this archeological site are mainly laterite and bricks constructions. Although the important places for exploring are mostly left ruins, but the remains are supported as the clues for historical evidences.

Kam Phaeng Phet Historical Park

- **Wat Phra Keaw wa**s found with a large temple area at the center of Kam Phaeng Phet Town. It was built about 600 years ago, in Sukhothai Period. The remained constructions of this temple gave plenty of clues for gathering the historical evidences of prospered Buddhism during Sukhothai Period, such as; the ordination halls, Viharns, and different styles of Stupas.

- **Wat Phra Thart was found with** a big pagoda built in Kam Phaeng Phet Style which was restored later.

- **Sa Mon was found with** the pool. It's believed that the pool was an ancient palace's location, also with many ancient artifacts and laterite base with some items of old constructions found here.

- **San Phra Isuan was found with Phra Isuan Statue made of bronze and shrine's base.** Phra Isuan or the Hindu God was a statue built to honor Brahms who performs religious royal ceremonies. The original statue is kept in Kam Phaeng Phet National Museum.

- Fortifications were found installed here; such as Chao Inth Fort, Moommuang Fort, and Wat Chang Fort.

- **Ghost Gate** was found with the gate of the size; 4 meter wide and 5.5 meter high, made of laterite within the inner wall. The Ghost Gate was the pathway for moving the body.

- **Wat Phranon was found** with laterite constructions and a bell-shape pagoda situated in this large temple areas.

- **Wat Phra Si Iriyabot** was found with a perfect of a huge standing Buddha remained and also found ruins of Buddha Statues which built in Sukhothai Style.

- ❖ **Wat Singh was found its location** next to Wat Si Iriyabot with the sculpture of lion at the front door platform remained.

- ❖ **Wat Chang Rop** was found on the highest land of this park with a very beautiful elephant statues built around the hall. "Chang" means "Elephant".

- ❖ **Wat Tabak Koo wa**s found at outer wall, with the big Viharn Hall and some of monks' house in the temple.

- ❖ **Wat Phe Ka Ram** was found at outer wall, with five bell-shaped pagodas and the Sema around. "Sema" is the sign showing of the ordination hall's boundary, usually built 4 Semas.

- ❖ **Wat Makok** was only found its boundary for buildings.

- ❖ **Wat Maklet was** found the base of the main pagoda and Viharn's base left only bricks in the temple.

- ❖ **Wat Arwas Yai was** found with the wall and its high lift base with ruined pagodas.

- ❖ **Wat Kam Phaeng Ngam wa**s found with ruined pagodas which built in round shape pagodas and large bases.

- ❖ **Wat Kru Si Hong was** found with the ordination hall, pagodas left ruins and monks' houses.

- ❖ **Wat Chedi Klom**; Chedi Klom means Round - Shape Pagoda, the plan of this temple was found in rectangle shape, made of laterite. The hall, round-shape pagodas, pagodas, pavilions and a pool were found left ruins.

- ❖ Visit **Kam Phaeng Phet National Museum** in town.

❑ Admire a beautiful Pagoda at **Wat Phra Borommathat Jediyaram**; one of the old temple in town (about 700 years old), known as Nakhon Choom Town. The huge pagoda contains Buddha's Relic, which is the sacred site for all Buddhists here. This is the center for many festivals in Kam Phaeng Phet.

Enjoy walking around **Nakhon Choom Community**; the old style homes and markets locate nearby the Wat Phra Borommathat Jediyaram.

❑ Try some nice Thai local food, taste local bananas (small size bananas taste sweet) and try famous grass jelly dessert of Cha Kang Rao called "Chao Guay", its black jelly come with syrup and ground ice, great for hot day!

❑ Discover the Center of Learning Buddhist Amulets Making in town. Kam Phaeng Phet is famous for Buddhist amulets-making because the soil here is rich with minerals. DIY Handmade Buddhist amulet for your own gift and souvenirs.

❑ Discover a cool place, **"Chong Yen";** it's the hilltop of Klong Lan where the cool fresh air is all year round. It's about 28 kms. from the entrance of **Mae Wong National Park** with abundant forests and rivers natural surroundings. It locates in Klong Lan District and a popular park for camping.

❑ Splash at a large basin **of Namtok Klong Lan at Klong Lan National Park.** The park is a highland with elevation 1,439 M. There are many waterfalls in this forest but the favorites for tourists are Klong Lan Waterfall and Klong Suan Mak Canal; for some challenging rapids in November. Let's go to Sukhothai.

SUKHOTHAI

Figure 135 Sukhothai

❑ Sukhothai was an early kingdom in the upper central region which heading to the north. The ruins of this old former capital city are designated a UNESCO Cultural World Heritage Site which is named as Sukhothai Historical Park and Associated Historic Town.

The historical park also includes Si Satchanalai and Kam Phaeng Phet Historical Park.

❑ The hundred of stone inscriptions of historical records of the Sukhothai Kingdom were found and called as "Sila Jaruek".

Sukhothai; a large kingdom, was the first capital of Siam, from the stone inscriptions; it's a rich and developed kingdom where it was the trade center and the origin of Sangkhalok Earthenware. Besides; the Thai arts and cultures included with Thai alphabets were started here.

❑ Sukhothai seems to be a land of memory and pride, we can't forget the importance of this great city and there are no doubts that, it's one of the popular tourist destinations.

SUKHOTHAI HISTORICAL PARK

❑ Explore **Sukhothai Historical Park;** the major part of Historic Town of Sukhothai and Associated Historic Towns; a cultural world heritage of UNESCO.

The location of this Historical Park is opposite to **Sukhothai National Museum** which is about 12 kilometers from downtown.

❑ The area of this former and prosperous capital city was found about 70 km^2, covered of many important palaces, temples and city walls.

❑ The bicycles are for hire here and tram is also available for tourist groups for sight-seeing around this large old town.

According to the historical evidences from archaeologists' exploration, more than two hundred ancient places and items found within this areas.

Sukhothai Historical Park and the ruins of this ancient kingdom are located on a foothill with a rectangle-shaped landscape, surrounded by the three layers of city rampart; the size found about 1300 meter wide and 1800 meter long with moats around the city walls.

❑ The **Sukhothai City Walls was** called as **"Tribul";** means the three-layer wall, described in one of Ram Kham Haeng Inscriptions or Ram Kham Haeng Stele or "Sila Jaruek". The stone inscriptions are kept in Bangkok National Museum. The city wall found is now located at Muang Kao Sub-district.

Figure 136 Silajaruek, The stone Inscription

Figure 137 Por Khun Ram Kham Haeng

❑ See the statue of **Por Khun Ram Kham Haeng Maharaj**; the memorial for the Great King of Sukhothai Kingdom. He was the king who created the Thai Alphabets and prospered the kingdom during his reign (1279-1298).

"Por" means "Father"; the king was called "Father" because of his kindness in ruling the kingdom like, a father takes good care of his children, by reaching the people by allowing them to file a complaint directed to him, expanded the kingdom and improved the quality of living by development of education, initiations of utilities and commerce within the kingdom.

❑ **Wat Mahathart** was the royal temple with royal graveyard, located at the center of Sukhothai Kingdom.

Figure 138 Phra Attharos at Wat Mahathat, Sukhothai

Please walk around and admire many stupas, halls, Viharns and Mondops in the temple area.

- ❖ **Viharn Hall** is a large building for religious service and ceremonies. It's like a multi purpose building of the temple. Viharn is normally called by Buddhists as any building in temple except the ordination hall.
- ❖ **The ordination hall** is called "Ubosoth" or "Bosth" which is the most important building; for performing ordination ritual and monk's Patimokkha; with Pali chanting for 227 rules of monk's disciplines on Buddha's Day. There are Sema with the ordination hall for noticing. Sema are the signs to indicate the boundary for the hall.

- ❑ **Wat Chanasongkram** was found with a large bell-shaped pagoda at the center.
- ❑ **Noen Prasart** was found with a large base of building in rectangle shape high-lifted with stairways at the front and the back of the area.
- ❑ **The City Shrine** was found a square - shaped base left ruined.
- ❑ **Wat Kham Phaeng Lang** was found with a group of small bases around near Wat Mahathat.
- ❑ **Wat Trakuan** was found with a principal pagoda and the base of ordination hall with waterway.
- ❑ **Wat Sorasak** was found with a large pagoda with 24 elephant sculptures decorated around.
- ❑ **Wat Trapangsau**; "Trapang" means pool, Trapangsau was one of the pools among the three within the Sukhothai Kingdom. The temple was named from the pool name. This temple was found with some of pagoda bases and halls within the areas.
- ❑ **Wat Son Kow** was found with a pagoda without the peak, some areas of the ordination hall and Mondop.
- ❑ **San Ta Pha Daeng** was found with a single pavilion of Khmer (Cambodian) style made of laterite.
- ❑ **Wat Sa Sri** was found with a very beautiful ancient temple building which situated at the middle of a large pool, which left only a big bell-shape pagoda and its surroundings.
- ❑ **Wat Trapang Gnoen** was found with a beautiful pagoda and Buddha Statue.
- ❑ **Wat Sri Sawai** was found with the three **Prangs**; ("Prang" is called for a dome shape of Shrine built in Khmer Style, look alike corn shape.), hall bases and some sculptures of graven images.

- **Wat Chetupon** was found outside the city wall, the remained temple seen with the statues of Buddha in four positions; standing, sitting, reclining and walking.
- **Wat Chang Lom** was found outside the city wall with a big pagoda, a square base decorated with elephant statues.

Figure 139 Wat Chang Lom, Sukhothai

Figure 140 Wat Taphan Hin, Sukhothai

❑ Admire a beautiful Huge Standing Buddha at **Wat Taphan Hin or Saphan Hin;** located outside the city wall at the west, situated on the hill in the forest, walk from the ground to the top about 300 meters.

❑ **Wat Chedi Si Hong** was found about 100 meters from Wat Chetupon with a big pagoda and some sculptures of people wore in different costumes.

❑ **Wat Sri Pijit Khirathi Kanlayaram** was found outside the city wall with the bell-shaped pagoda built on the high-lifted base.

❑ **Wat Chedi Soong** was found outside the city wall with a very tall pagoda with the height about 33 meters.

- **Wat Trapang Thong Lang** was found outside the city wall with many important architectures and sculptures such as, Mondop, Viharn and Stupas. (Stupa is a mound-like or pagoda-like used for keeping the ashes of monk or the important people, Pagoda is where The Buddha's Relic enshrined)
- **Wat Phra Pai Luang** was found at the north of Sukhothai City wall, with many constructions since the beginning of Sukhothai was the capital city and also found the ancient architectures of three halls surrounded with some of sculptural items.
- **Tao Tu Liang** was found with the group of 63 porcelain kilns outside the city wall.
- **Wat Sri Chum** was found outside the city wall with the huge Buddha Statue kept inside a mondop and faded Lanka Art painting on the wall.

Figure 141 Wat Sri Chum

SI SATCHANALAI HISTORICAL PARKS

Figure 142 Si Satchanalai Historical Park, Sukhothai

Satchanalai Historical Park is part of the Historic Town, located at Si Satchanalai District in Sukhothai.

The plan of the park is by Yom Riverside surrounded by three mountains like, a natural fortress; by Khao Phra Sri, Khao Bat and Khao Yai. The inside walls was found with laterite constructions and earth wall, included with retaining wall layout and also surrounded by moats along the walls.

The total area of this park is about 45 square kilometers; with 281 historical sites were found.

It's about 50 kilometers from Sukhothai downtown, heading to Sawan Kalok district.

- **Wat Chedi Chet Taew** was found with many stupas built in many art styles such as, Lotus Bud-Shape, Castle-Shape and Bell-Shape, standing in rows within the temple areas.
- **Wat Suan Keaw Autthayan Yai** was found it was one of the important temple of Si Satchanalai Kingdom, with a rectangle layout, a large pagoda in bell-shape made of laterite but left with base, the main hall with 7 stairways, some of the principal Buddha bases and the monk seats left in the temple.
- **Wat Nang Phraya** was found with the main stupa in bell-shaped surrounded by the elephant sculptures. The design of stucco patterns of the temple becomes inspiration for gold jewelry craftsmen here.
- **Wat Chang Lom was found** the elephant sculptures around the big pagoda base. "Chang Lom" means "Elephants Around". It was a large temple of Si Satchanalai built in the reign of King Ram Kam Haeng.
- **Wat Lak Muang** was found near the palace inside city wall, with the principal Stupa built in Khmer Style, viharn base and mondop.
- **Wat Na Wang** was found with the hall base made of laterite in rectangle shape of about 4 room size and a front room of the hall.
- **The Royal Palace** was found with the palace ground; from the archaeologist's excavation found that there were many ancient items; like, roof tiles, stoneware, pool, ruins of buildings, etc. in this area.
- **Wat Suan Kaew Autthayan Noi** was found nearby the palace. It's assumed that, the temple was the royal temple before. The big principal stupa surrounded by small stupas and a statue of Buddha inside the mondop were found in the temple.
- **Wat Khao Suwanna Khiri** was found with the outstanding pagoda on the top of the hill.

- **Wat Khao Phanom Ploeng** was found on the top of a hill at the center of Si Satchanalai Kingdom with 114 stairsteps. The ruined pagodas, ordination hall with Buddha statue in sitting position and a mondop at the back of this temple were found here.

- **Wat Kudi Rai** was found outside the city wall, on the river bank of Yom River. The temple was found with viharn building of 4 rooms; inside having some monk seats left, mondop behind this viharn having the statue of Buddha in sitting position and the main hall.

- **Tuliang Kiln** Education and Conservation Center of Pa Yang Village; 26 kilns found spreading around the Yom Riverside, the exploration of these kilns found bricks on mounds for making food containers like, cups and bowls.

- **Wat Noi Jumpee** was found outside the wall. The temple was found with the laterite round-shaped pagoda and the only viharn building which left the floor with glazed tiles.

- **Wat Chom Chuen and archaeological excavation site of Wat Chom Chuen were** on Yom Riverside. The temple was found with Viharn Hall of 6 rooms situated in front of the laterite bell-shaped Stupa and a Mondop.

- **Wat Thung Setthi was found** the layout of the temple in rectangle area made of laterite with 4 entrances, with a laterite bell-shaped pagoda, square-shaped pillars and many surrounding pagoda bases in the temple.

For those who have more days here, you can explore more of places in Sukhothai Province.

- Camping at **Doi Khao Moong** at Si Satchanalai District and enjoy a nice view of "Sea of Fog" early in the morning.

❑ If you ride a train to Sukhothai and choose to stop at **Sawankalok Train Station, you will see** more than 100 years old wooden building of this station with a gallery of old items exhibited and it's nice to walk around here.

If you come to Sukhothai by plane, **Sawankalok District is an interesting place you should not miss. It's about** 38 kilometers from Sukhothai. It's once the important port center for trades in the past.

❑ Discover the **Street of Art**; where there are many artworks from different Asian Artists nearby the Sawankalok Train Station.

❑ Discover an ancient style wooden building of **the old Sawankalok Police Station** since World War II. The station was built in "Panyah"style which was a European style Building with tile-roof slope like, pyramid without gable. The old station now becomes the museum for displaying some of the things and information for this police station and the Sawankalok Town in the past.

❑ Taste a famous delicious food; Noodle of Sukhothai; a kind of noodle with different ingredients from other places.

❑ Visit **Ban Na Ton Jun**; a local village homestay and join activities with villagers. You can see their local products and the local huts.

❑ Visit the Gallery of **Sankhalokware** and get one for souvenir such as, stoneware, earthenware, ceramic, etc . Sankalokware is a famous earthenware district of Sukhothai Province.

❑ Adventure in a beautiful landscape of **Ram Kam Haeng National Park**; this park is full of ancient ruins surrounded by forests, the areas covers three districts; Dan Lan Hoi, Khiri Math and Muang Districts of Sukhothai. It's about 30 kilometers from downtown.

Figure 143 Sangkhalok Ware, Sukhothai

❑ Hike at **Khao Luang Trail**; it's the highest mountain in Sukhothai located in Ram Kam Haeng National Park and enjoy exploring caves, waterfalls, water reservoir, and see many herbal plants forest.

❑ Bike at **Thung Saliam;** one of the districts belongs to Sukhothai where located about 68 kilometers from downtown, admire a nice view of rice fields and local living. It's not well known among tourists yet but there are many interesting places, such as beautiful temples and a scenic view here. The temples you will see in Thung Saliam are:

❑ Wat Pipatmongkon
  ❑ Wat Klangdong
  ❑ Wat Thung Saliam
  ❑ Wat Mae Thulau

❑ Visit **Ban Thung Luang;** a village in Khirimat District where is well known of earth ware pottery. You will see the demonstration of making local earth wares by the village community which is a unique art of handmade product.

PITSANULOK

Figure 144 Phra Phuttha Chinnarat, Pitsanulok

❏ Pitsanulok is called "Muang Song Kwae" by locals. It was established 600 years ago, located at the middle between the central region and the north region of Thailand.

Many Thai people visit here, with the purpose for paying respect to **Phra Phuttha Chinnaraj;** the principal Buddha Statue, this landmark of Pitsanulok situated at the hall of **Wat Phra Si Rattana Mahathat.**

The Nan River flows through the middle of Pitsanulok Town from north to south; divide the land into two parts of the river bank.

The distance from Bangkok to the province is about 380 kilometers. Transportation: by rail; to Pitsanulok Station, buses; at the Northern Bus Terminal at Morchit.

The tourists, who travel to the north, choose to stop overnight here and some of them fly directly here for sight-seeing in the province areas.

When you firstly arrive in Pitsanulok, you must visit some temples in town for learning of the history and the locals.

❑ The landmark of this province is one of the sacred Buddha Statue   s in Thailand which is named **"Phra Phuttha Chinnaraj". The statue was** assumed were made in 1357 during Sukhothai Period and kept inside Viharn Hall of **Wat Phra Si Rattana Mahathat** or called by local "Wat Yai" which situated at the west of the temple.

The figure of this Buddha image is one of the most beautiful sculpture in Thailand and also very popular for modeling in making Buddha Statues in many temples.

The statue was original made of bronze; later was cladded with gold sheets in 1602 during Ayutthaya Period.

In 1901, King Rama V ordered to build the Principal Buddha Statue for The Marble Temple or Wat Benjama Borpit in Bangkok by modeling from Phra Phuttha Chinnaraj in Pitsanulok.

There is a Tradition for worshipping Phra Phuttha Chinnaraj on Maka Pucha Day which is on the Full Moon Day of the Third Month (Buddhist Calendar), and become an annual festival day in Pitsanulok.

❑ Admire the old pagoda in **Wat Phra Si Rattana Mahathat**. The pagoda was assumed about 600 years old and Buddha's Relic was kept inside. You can walk around to see the museum of the temple. You can see two more temples in this temple's areas; **Wat Ratchaburana and Wat Nang Phraya.**

- ❑ **Wat Ratchaburana is** on the west of Nan River Bank. It was the assumed that the temple built since Sukhothai Period but restored many times. It's announced as a national archaeological site in 1936.
- ❑ Walk **to Wat Nang Phraya;** a temple which is famous for the origin of "Phra Nang Phraya Amulets". The Buddha amulets were found within the temple and become the legend among Thai Buddhist worshippers.

It's assumed that, Wat Nang Phraya was named from the queen's name. She's the mother of King Naresuan, the Great, of Ayutthaya Period.

The evidences found that she made plenty of the Buddha image amulets by following the old tradition for merits and kept all of them inside the pagoda at Wat Ratchaburana. The amulets were buried for a long, long time and the temple also was abandoned until they were found from excavation in 1901. The image of Buddha-amulets looked very beautiful and made Wat Nang Phraya becomes the famous temple of "Phra Nang Phraya".

- ❑ Adventure in **Thung Salang Luang National Park;** this park is called as "Savannah of Thailand", the land is with a grassland which color changed by the seasons. It locates at Noen Ma Prang District. If you have a chance to explore Pitsanulok Province, you must try camping or trailing in the park for admiring many wonderful places and exciting activities such as; **Tham Duen Tham Dao;** one of the beautiful caves in Thailand with a stream running through the cave. You can explore by walking for about 1.4 kms. to see the beauty of stalactites and stalagmites coated with silica minerals glittering around the cave when the light shines on.

❖ **Thung Nang Phraya Muang Laen**

❖ **Khaeng Sopa Waterfall**

"Khaeng" means "Rapids"

❖ **Khaeng Wang Nam Yen**; the white water rapids with plenty of big rocks in the middle of river, and it's where fresh -water jelly-fish and rare butterflies are found.
❖ **Saphan Saling**; the sling bridge across the Khek River.
❖ **Thung Non Son Field.**
❖ **Tham Phra Wang Daeng; is** 13.5 kilometer long, the largest and the longest cave in Thailand with a river inside the cave.
❑ Explore **Tham Pha Ta Phon No Hunting Area;** it's the Wild Animal Conservation Group Management Office of Department of National Parks, the area is within the boundary of **Pa Lum Num Wangthong** situated at Noen Maprang District.

The total area is about 2,840,000 square meters and about 85 kilometers from Pitsanulok downtown. The landscapes of the park are mostly limestone hills with steep cliffs include two rivers runs through it. The areas seem to have water all year round which is quiet rarely found in Thailand.

❑ There are many attractions like caves, fossil points and Japanese Script Point for exploring. Let's explore Tham Pha Ta Phon: ("Tham" means "Cave").

Tham Pha Ta Phon No Hunting Area

❖ **Discover a beautiful cave at Tham Naresuan;** a beautiful cave with stalagmites, stalactites, lime plasters walls and pillar formations. There are many kinds of bats live here, so the cave was announced as a Natural and Environment Heritage Site in 1989.

- **Tham Roea is** a long cave of about 1,400 meters, "Roea" means "Boat". On the cave's ceiling, found a formation of overturned boat.
- **Tham Tao;** it's found with a large hall inside this cave.
- **Tham Lod;** is a cave where there are waterways from the stream in front of the cave and flow inside also.
- **Tham Pha Daeng;** is a large cave with red color on the cliffs.
- **Tham Pha Ta Phon No Hunting Area**
- The natural beauty of **Tham Kang Kao** is still pure and strange. "Kang Kao" means "Bat". It is a large cave with steep steps inside so it's quiet difficult to get in.
- Discover **Fossil Point;** it's assumed that, here was the sea with many animals living since 360 million years ago.
- **Japanese Script Point** was told by the legend that Japanese Army settled here during World War II and found with cryptic puzzles on the rocks.

☐ Adventure in **Charttrakarn Waterfall National Park** in Charttrakarn and Nakhonthai Districts. The park is the mountainous areas; having the highest point about 1,277 meters above the sea level at **Phu Gai Hoi.** It is full of forests and streams with high humidity climate. There are many attractions found here:

- **Chattrakarn Waterfall;** splash in this 7-tier waterfall within natural beautiful surroundings.
- **Na Jarn Waterfall** is 9-tier waterfall and with amazing species of butterflies and insects around the areas.
- **Namtok Pha Khu Kham** is a 50 meter-single fall waterfall.

- ❖ **Chang Luang Hill**
- ❖ **Pha Kradan Lek** is the cliff with pre-historic carvings.
- ❖ **Pha Daeng** is the steep red cliff caused by erosion of the red sandstone naturally; "Daeng" means "Red".
- ❖ **Footprints** of ancient animals found on the sandstone cliffs.
- ❖ **Pha Phueng Roi Rung**; "Phueng Roi Rung" means 100 hives; it's a hundred - hive cliff.

Figure 145 Phu Soi dao, Pitsanulok

❑ **Explore Phu Soi Dao National Park** in
Chartrakarn District

❑   The park covers rich forest of two provinces which are Pitsanulok and Uttraradit. It's the 4th highest peak in Thailand, with 2,102 meters above sea level and the climate here is cold all year round.

❑   Discover a very beautiful orchid flowers and variety of flowers and plants at **Ban Rom Klao Pitsanulok Botanic Garden by Royal Initiative** located in Chartrakarn District.

The land was abandoned land and a part of The Ban Rom Klao Battlefield in the past. Her Majesty the Queen Sirikit (in the reign of King Rama 9) started the project to develop the land and initiated an agency for conserving highland plant species in order to conserve forests and to support villagers to have a better life quality. The place has a very nice view for camping.

Figure 146 Phu Hin Long Klah, Pitsanulok

☐ Adventure at **Phu Hin Long Klah** in Nakhonthai District. The area was a historical significance for being the land where the communist groups hid and performed their activities. The weather is quiet cold here during dry season (October-February). There are places for camping and quiet popular among tourists because the landscape is similar to the northern region.

☐ Discover **Flag-Pole Cliff** which is about 1,614 meter high. Nature trail along the jungle to the top of the cliff for looking at an amazing view of mountain ranges during sunset. It was the site where the Communist Party of Thailand raised their flag; the red background with hammer and sickle symbols, to show the victory over the Military.

PHICHIT

Figure 147 Phichit

❑ Phichit is a province nearby Pitsanulok, located in the lower northern region of Thailand. It takes about 5 hours to Phichit by car and the distance is about 350 Kms. from Bangkok. Driving by passing Nakhon Sawan and turn right to Pitsanulok route to Phichit.

This province borders Petchaboon and Kham Phaeng Phet. The public transports to Phichit are buses at the Northern Bus Station at Mo Chit near Jatujak Park and rails to 10 stations in Phichit; to Wang Klang, Bang Moon Nak, Ho Krai, Dong Tha Kop, Tha Phan Hin, Huay Kate, Hua Dong, Wang Krod, Phichit and Tha Lor Stations.

"Chalawan, Long- Boat Racing Tradition, Wat Tha Luang, Bueng Si Fai, Historical Park, Woven Fabric..........." Let's explore Phichit.

Most Thai tourists visit Phichit for The Annual Long-Boat Racing Tradition. It's an exciting race where audience enjoys with both watermen and the voice over. The rowing competitions are on Nan River; the biggest long-boat racetrack in Thailand and the start point is by **Wat Tha Luang** during the beginning of September, in the rainy season.

The main river of Phichit Province is **Nan River** which is originated from Luang Phra Bang Mountain in Nan Province in the north of Thailand. The river's length is about 740 kms. which flows through many provinces. Phichit is named "Chalawan Town"; which come from The Giant Crocodile in the legend.

THE LEGEND OF CHALAWAN, THE GIANT CROCODILE OF NAN RIVER IN PHICHIT

- Once upon a time, there's a couple lived nearby Nan River and earned by fishing. They found crocodile's egg in a pool during fishing and kept the egg home until it's hatched from the egg.

- The couple loved this little crocodile very much and raised it as their child by keeping it in a pool nearby home. It grew up very fast and ate more food.

- The food given for the big crocodile were only fish and small water animals which were not enough for it. It killed the couple and ate them for its food finally.

- After the couples were eaten, the crocodile then moved to Nan River which was about 500 meters from the couple's home.

- The crocodile seemed to be the "King" of the Nan River, from its huge size. It was rampant by taking people in the river areas for its food. The people gave its name "Chalawan".
- One day a millionaire's daughter was taken by this crocodile when she was standing by the river. He announced to the people in the whole town for finding a hero who could kill Chalawan. Whoever was the hero would be rewarded with the other daughter and his treasure.
- The merchant from Nonthaburi; named Kraithong dived into the river and could beat the giant Chalawan down with a sacred lance finally.
- It's assumed that, a large cave situated in the middle of Nan River where the huge crocodile could stay.
- It's been recounted the tale of Chalawan's size; from the head to tail was the width of a large canal.
- The legend was also become a drama depicted by the King Rama II and it has been told until nowadays.

Figure 148 Phichit Town

❏ Ride a train to Phichit Station and admire this old style railway station. It was established the same time as Hua Lum Phong Railway Station in 1907.

❏ Walk around the Claw Tree Skywalk.

❏ Admire **"Luang Por Peth"**; the principal Buddha Statue in Phra Viharn of **Wat Tha Luang**; the temple is situated on Nan River Bank.

The annual festival here is The Celebration Day of Worshipping Luang Por Peth Buddha and the same time as the Long-Boat Racing Festival here. The festival is known as one of the popular events in Thailand for Thai tourists and makes them travel directly here in about September-October; it will be announced by the province.

If you are close to this province, you may experience this exciting Long-Boat Racing in Phichit.

❑ Explore the Old Phichit City; it's a National Heritage Park located about 7 kms from downtown. The location was found that, it's established since 1058. The Old Town consists of ruins of City Wall, Moats, Pagodas, Stupas, etc.

By walking around the park areas, you will also see the City Shrine, Wat Mahathat; the old national heritage; found with many pagodas, stupas and ordination hall built in Sukhothai and Ayutthaya Period, Chalawan Cave; a cavity covered by the soil collapsed. The sculptural crocodile; Chalawan and Kraithong were made from the legend. There's also **Ko Simala,** a pile of soil forming like an island outside the city wall.

❑ Admire a panorama viewpoint on the top floor of **Wat Khao Roob Chang**; the temple where a beautiful pagoda built in Lanka Style located on the top of a hill. It's about 15 kms from town.

➢ **Bueng Si Fai is** a large oxbow lake of Nan River, situated 1 kilometer from the city hall. It's the 5th largest lake of Thailand; the 1st is Bueng Borrapeth, then Nong Harn Lake, Bueng La Han and Kwan Phayao. There are many nice places for exploring such as; **Suan Somdej Phra Sri Nakarin**; a place for walking around and watch the beautiful sunset. **Chalawan Statue** ; the sculptural giant Crocodile from the legend; its size here is 38 meter long, 6 meter wide and 5 meter high, with a conference room built inside the crocodile sculpture. **Aquarium,** Pavilions in the lake, Crocodile Pools and Ground Drawing of Chalawan and waterfall in three-dimensional space.

❑ Walk around the old market of Phichit; Wang Krod Community Market, see the old theater, houses and Chinese Shrine.

❑ **Discover** the learning center **of Vietnamese in Thailand at Ban Dong Ho Chi Minh Museum in Phichit Town,** where the exhibition of old notebook written by Mr. Ho Chi Minh with his personal appliances include the model of his home in Vietnam.

The former Vietnamese leader made this place for political activities with his fellows for trying to salvage freedom to Vietnam.

❑ Visit **Tha Lor,** the more than 100 year old Thai-Chinese community, where you can see the old school and Chinese shrine. You should taste the old local dessert of these areas.

Figure 149 Boat Racing

PHETCHABUN

❑ Phetchabun is a popular province during cool season. It's a place for camping and admires a beautiful temple on the hill which is called Wat Phrathart Pha Son Kaew.

It's about 350 kilometers from Bangkok. The best time for visiting is in November-February. It's a nice province for refreshing during weekend. Many Thai tourists choose here instead of going to the north as for relaxing with family because it's near Bangkok.

The transports to Pethchaboon are cars or buses at The Northern Bus Terminal at Mo Chit, Booking the Package Tours and plane. You will enjoy picturesque scenery along the curvy roads and drink fresh air there.

❑ Explore **Khao Kho** National Park; a newly national park located in Khao Kho District, the north of Phetchaboon. This park is full of various kinds of forests and wildlife and also with beautiful landscape of mountains, forest, caves, streams and waterfalls.

❑ It's a part of the historical battleground between Thai Communist Party and the Royal Thai Army in 1965-1984.

❑ I came here without intention for this province but I chose the way back from the north trip to Bangkok by this route. The road was not so good that time but I found that it's such a good place for relaxing and getting fresh air like, in the north. It's one of popular choices for Thai tourists during cool season.

❑ Khao kho is not only remarkable for picturesque scenery but also well known of a beautiful temple built from unique imagination where we feel that, we are entering into "heaven" on this earth.

❑ This temple is called **Wat Phrathat Pha Sorn Kaew;** a beautiful of Buddhist Arts of Faith Architecture; with the stunning of Huge Five

Buddhas Statues on the mountaintop sanctuary of tranquility which is full of amazing design.

❑ Walking around the temple areas for admiring such details of art in the decorations of pagodas, halls, pavilions, gardens and floors. It's incredible to see this kind of arts among the valleys with nature surroundings. Must visit!

❑ Discover the amazing viewpoint of 360 degrees in Wat Phrathat Pha Sorn Kaew.

❑ Discover a wonderful and peaceful place for learning Dhamma and meditation in Wat Phrathat Pha Sorn Kaew; the abbot of the temple allows people who would like to learn Dhamma from Buddha's Teaching, you can stay temporary in houses of the temple.

- ❑ Chill in a café of Campson Sub-district.
- ❑ Admire a sea of fog and mountain-view with Kho Tree in the very early morning at **Wat Khong Niem; it's** a temple with a good viewpoint for sea clouds.
- ❑ Admire a panorama view of Khao Kho District at **Khao Takian Scenic Spot.**
- ❖ **See Phra Thamnak Khao Kho; which** is a palace situated on the hill. It's built on **Khao Ya Hill** for expressing the gratitude to The King Rama 9th and the Queen. The location of this palace becomes one of the most beautiful viewpoints of Phetchabun. This palace was built later after the war; the fighting with communist group at that time. King Bhumibol and Queen Sirikij came here; with their morale support, for visiting military base and people in Khao Kho District during the fight with the communist group.

The palace was on the hilltop; with 1100 meters above the sea level, where there are places nearby allowed for camping and enjoying the hills surroundings.

Reach the **Khao Kho Summit**; the highest point of Khao Kho at 1143 above sea level.

- ❖ Discover a military museum; about 1 kilometer from the summit areas, displays military vehicles and weapons used in the base.
- ❖ See the Khao Kho Memorial; to honor all lost people and soldiers during the fight against the communist group in the past and stop by the market of local products then you should visit **Khao Kho Wind Farm**; the largest wind turbines in Thailand.

❖ Trail to **Than Thip Waterfall**; a single tier waterfall about 26 meter high and 30 meter wide, a famous beautiful waterfall of Phetchabun Province.

❑ Explore **Si Thep Historical Park**; the ancient city in Si Thep District, away from downtown 130 kilometers. Walk around the park and admire many Prangs, halls, caves, shrine and pagodas.

• Trail along stream for 2 kilometers from the car park of **Tat Mok** National Park Office for refreshing and splashing at the beautiful Tat Mok and Song Nang Waterfalls. This Tat Mok National Park is a small park; located about 40 kilometers from Phetchabun Town where you can have a nice viewpoint of the province.

• One of the popular destinations for Petchabun is Phu Tab Berg; a picturesque highland of Lom Kao District where the highest mountain in Petchabun is; its height is about 1,768 meters. I came to a temple here long-time ago and stayed overnight in cold weather of the forest.

Figure 150 Phu TabBerg

TAK

Figure 151 Thung Yai Naresuan

☐ Tak is a province on the way to the north. When we ride close to Tak, we can notice scenery of mountains and forests. It's a province for not only stop a while but there are so many beautiful places you must explore.

• Tak locates in a central area by the upper west of Thailand, close to Myamar. Moei River is like, a border line between the two countries.

- Tak was a battlefront town in the history since Sukhothai Period. The land in Tak Province is the 4th largest of Thailand but the population here is the 2nd least of the country. The distance from Bangkok is about 400 kilometers. Flights are available to Tak and Mae Sot Airports. Bus and trains are convenient from anywhere
- ❑ Adventure in Thungyai Naresuan of Thungyai-Huai Kha Khaeng Wildlife Sanctuaries; a UNESCO Natural World Heritage Site in Thailand which covers in many provinces include The **Um Phang Wildlife Sanctuary National Park** in Tak.

This park is a part **of Thungyai Naresuan Wildlife Santuary in Kanchanaburi** which connects to the south of Tak Province. "Naresuan" is the name of King Naresuan the Great. He settled the Army Base in Tak during the war with Burma.

- ❏ Experience riding a car passing 1,219 curves along the road to Um Phang District. Stop at Luead Forest Ranger Station.Camping at Um Phang National Park is fun and fresh breath. Clean your lung here.

- ❏ **Pa La Tha Village**; an old village with old style of wooden houses. It's a place where you can take a ride inflatable-boat trip from the village. It takes about 3 hours along Mae Klong River for exploring such as, waterfalls, hot pool and forests through Pha

- ❏ **Trail at Um Phang Wildlife Sanctuary National Park** and pass by many waterfalls.

❑ Walking from the entrance of the park about 1.5 kms., you will discover **the stunning Thi Lo Su Waterfall. It's** the largest (about 5oo meter wide) and the highest (more than 2000 meter high) waterfall in Thailand with plenty of water in June-November. Booking a package tour for this adventure is more convenient. Thi Lau Su Waterfall is a beautiful creation on earth.

❑ Ride an elephant for exploring the nature along stream into the jungle from **Pa La Tha Village.**

Mae Sot District has an airport. It's away from Tak downtown about 85 kilometers to this border-checkpoint. The district is a special economic zone; as the center for trades between Thailand and Myanmar. You can fly to Mae Sot from Bangkok for sight-seeing inside the district and nearby such as;

❑ The golden pagoda at **Wat Chumpon Khiri**, the pagoda is 20 meter high, built by modeling from Chavedagong Pagoda in Myanmar,.

❑ Splash at **Namtok Pha Jaroen**; a large limestone waterfall of 97 tiers waterfall flows year round, located in Phop Phra District, away from Mae Sot Airport 40 minutes by car.

❑ Relax at Mae Kasa Hot Spring.

❑ Refresh at Namtok Thararak; a 30-meter high limestone waterfall in the rich forest.

❑ Eat Roti grilled in a jar, the old aged Roti and a signature of Mae Sot.

❑ Discover Blue Cave; an unseen cave with reflecting of natural blue color of mineral inside the cave.

❑ Chill at **Mon Mork Tawan**; a nice high hill; about 1100 meters above the sea level, located in Phop Phra District where the weather is cool all year round.

❑ Spa and massage at **Kasa Village**; in the middle of rice fields.

❑ Morning walk **at Pha Jaroen Market.**

❏ Discover the tallest and biggest tree in Thailand. It's called **Krabak Tree** or scientific name is called Anisoptera Costata. The size is 50 meter high and 16 meter wide. You have to trail about 2 kilometers in **Taksin Maharaj National Park.** See **San Chao Phra War**; a shrine along the Tak-Mae Sot Road.

❏ Discover **The Moei River the Westernmost Point** and enjoy shopping some stones; like, jade bracelets for nice souvenirs at local market here.

❏ Don't forget to visit Wat Thai Wattanaram, located near the Friendship Bridge Thai-Burmese of Moei River.

❏ Camping at **Mae Moei National Park** and see a beautiful sunrise. I came here in 1996 and stayed overnight in the forest park; it's a very good atmosphere in a small tent under the falling rain. The clouds covered all over the area. I remembered there were about 5 people camping there that time. It's not so convenient but we enjoyed the cold weather and silent night. We were tired from tough driving up to the highland here but staying in the nature and heard the sound of animals occasionally brought about impression anytime we thought of this mountainous area. Good old days!

Figure 152 Wat Thai Wattanaram

Figure 153 The entrance to Mae Usu Cave

❑ Discover a beautiful cave; Mae Usu at Mae Moei National Park. It's a hidden gem which has been known for its beauty inside the cave which is called "the theater under the Earth" by tourists. When I explored the cave, it was in 1996, I had to walk carefully because the water in the cave was above my knees, and the distance was about 300 meters. The adventure was quiet scared me because it's hard to guess what would be inside this cave. We were guided by the Karen Hill Tribe. It's very impressive when we saw amazing inside the cave; I thought that I was lost in another world, it's really the hidden gem in Tak.

KANCHANABURI

Figure 154The Bridge over the River Kwai, Kanchanaburi

Kanchanaburi was one of the important outposts in the war between Thai and Burmese Armies during The Ayutthaya Period. At present, Kanchanaburi is well known for The Bridge over The River Kwai; a part of "The Death Railway"; built in 1940-1944 during The World War II.

The railway route is 415 kilometers between Ban Pong in Ratchaburi Province to Than ba yu zayat in Burma. This railway was in Thai Zone around 304 Kilometers and crossed The Three Pagodas Pass and The River Kwai in Kanchanaburi. The estimated 100,000 allied POWs and Asian laborers were forced labor to construct the railway to supply troops and weapons in Burma Campaign of The World War II, caused almost all of the forced prisoners died from this horrific working conditions.

TRANSPORTS:

RAIL: Must try traveling by train from Bangkok to Kanchanaburi. You can check the rail routes from the website so you can get the train from the nearest station you are convenient.

BUS: At the Southern Bus Terminal.

ONE DAY TOUR/ PACKAGE TOURS
CAR OR TAXI METER

Figure 155 The Death Railway

❑ **The Bridge over The River Kwai** is the landmark of Kanchanaburi Province. You should walk along this historic bridge; about 300 meters for crossing the river.

❑ Discover **"The Death railway"** route by riding the train from Kanchanaburi Station to Nam Tok Station for about 77 Kilometers. The schedule of this train is everyday, but the schedule from Bangkok to Nam Tok Station is during Sat-Sun and Public Holidays. Please check from the website or train station at Hua Lum Phong or Bang Sue Railway Station.

❑ Discover the beautiful viewpoint of The River Kwai from **The Krasae Cave** by walking from Wang Pho Railway Station about 100 meters alongThe Death Railway track. (Watch out the train!)

❑ Visit Kanchanaburi War Cemetery or Don Ruk Cemetery; the main prisoner of World War II cemetery, of about 7000 POWs which mostly are Australian, British and Dutch buried.

❑ Visit **Chong Kai War Cemetery**; which situated on the bank of River Kwai Noi, known as the monument of POWs of World War II.

❑ Visit **JEATH Museum for** seeing the displays of photographs and some of illustrations telling the living condition from the prisoners of war (POWs).

❑ Visit **Ban Kao National Museum** in Kanchanaburi where the prehistoric antiquities were found in the province.

Figure 156 Prasart Muang Sing, Kanchanaburi,

❑ Explore **Prasart Muang Singh** Historical Park; the ancient park located on the bank of Kwai Noi River. The park was assumed to be about 800 years old. It's only about 43 kms from town and 6 kms from Ban Kao National Museum.

The park is the old ruined city built in Khmer or Cambodian architecture. The place was excavated and found prehistoric of human skeleton with metal tools and some instruments.

Prasart Muang Singh was repaired and developed by The Fine Arts Department to be a very beautiful place for visiting. There are signs of QR code of many languages for guiding you inside the archaeological site, a large layout of the Town Plan and the City Wall made of laterite.

- ❑ The Historical Site 1; Prasart Muang Singh, the ruins of Khmer Style of Prang, stupa and walls made of laterite.
- ❑ The Historical Site2; this site is laterite construction decorated with stucco left only base.
- ❑ The Historical Site3; located outside the area, see the ruins of brick and laterite bases.
- ❑ The Historical Site4; see the ruins in rectangle-shaped floor; look alike 4 room-building, made of laterite.
- ❑ Artifact Gallery; located near the parking lot, see many of architectural parts; like, terracotta stucco, stone and laterite from excavation.
- ❑ Prehistoric Human Skeleton Grave; there are four of skeletons found during excavation near Kwai Noi River.
- ❑ Guest House in the park for staying overnight.

Figure 157 The Three Pagoda Pass, Kanchanaburi

- ❑ Discover the end route of the west in Thailand at **The Three Pagodas Pass**; near the border of Myanmar. It's a historic site since Ayutthaya Period.
- ❑ The local market nearby The Three Pagodas Pass is interesting; you can shop for local souvenirs and see mostly people here have Burmese descent.
- ❑ Experience by crossing the border to Myanmar via The Three Pagodas Pass Checkpoint, just for looking around the town and visit some temples in Myanmar.
- ❑ Chill out and Relax on a Raft house nearby the River Kwai River and enjoy swimming and rafting in the river.
- ❑ Visit **the Hellfire Pass Memorial Museum; it's** where the prisoners of war were made to do forced labor 18 hrs a day for constructing the railway tracks to Burma by the orders from Japanese Troops during World War II. The atmosphere here reminds the visitors of the prisoners' sufferings from the dreadful injuries and diseases from this work condition at that time.

Figure 158 Hell Fire Pass, Kanchanaburi

- ❏ Swim in the beautiful **Erawan Waterfall at** Erawan National Park; a popular destination for all tourists during weekend. It's seven-tiered waterfall with a large natural pool for swimming on the second tier. It's only 65 kms from Kanchanaburi downtown.

- ❏ Trekking on **Chang Phueak Mountain** (during October- February) for 8 kilometers (takes about 6 hrs.) and stay overnight on the mountain at the tent ground. Please contact the Thong Pha Phum National Park for the adventure-activities.

- ❏ **Lam Khlong Ngu National Park** is one of amazing park of Kanchanaburi at Thong Pha Phum District. The park, caves and waterfall are preserved and protected area of Department of National Parks, Wildlife and Plant Conservation. The cave has the highest monolithic (by nature) in the world. Its height is 62.5 meters.

❑ See the beautiful scenery of Vachiralongkorn Dam or Khao Laem Dam; the first concrete-faced rock-fill dam in Thailand supplies a 300 MW hydroelectric power station with water. It's built in 1979 and started filling with water in 1884. The dam lies across Kwai Noi River located in Thong Pha Phum District.

Figure 159 The wooden Bridge, Kanchanaburi

❑ Discover the longest wooden bridge in Thailand and the second of the world at **Sang Khra Buri;** the charming town of simple living, with scenic views of nature surroundings.

Figure 160 The Sunken Temple, Kanchanaburi

- Discover the Temple of **Luang Por Utthama** or the former name was called Wang Wiwekaram Monastery which gets drowned under the lagoon of Vajiralongkorn Dam for 27 years, appear the beauty of the old shrine whenever tide is low, about March – April. It's known as the sunken temple. The temple was built in 1954 by the former abbot of the temple; Luang Por Utthama, and people here. When the dam was finished in 1984, the water was flooded to the temple and the nearby areas. The abbot moved some of the items away to the new temple on the hill and left the ordination hall sunk into the water during the high tide season. You can walk in the hall in March which is the low tide season to see the ruined interior of the wall and its stunning appearance. Some of tourists dived under the water for admiring during the high tide period and some of them hire the speed boat to see this sunken hall in the dam.

- The popular photo-spot is at amazing giant Rain Tree or Samanea saman or "Chamchuri" called as Thai name, approximately 100 years old, spreading its branches with about 25 meter wide and 20 meter tall, at Koh Samrong District. If you are fond of posting a beautiful photo, you should add this one on your lists.

❑ Discover the largest model of The Royal Barge and the Old Boat Museum **at Wat Sa Long Ruea,** the old temple of Ayutthaya Period in Kanchanaburi.

❑ Explore Kanchanaburi more to see the **Sai Yok Yai waterfall** by riding speed boat.

❑ Discover one of the most beautiful waterfalls in Thailand which is called**"Nam Tok Huay Mae Khamin"** at Srisawat District in Kanchanaburi.

"Namtok" means "Waterfall"

Figure 161 Mae Khamin waterfall

RATCHABURI

Figure 162 Ratchaburi

Ratchaburi means "The land of King". It's where one of the most famous tourist attractions **"Damnoen Saduak Floating Market"** located. This floating market is known and listed for a "must" tour in Thailand while many of them haven't known where it is.

Dragon jar is also put in the quote for Ratchaburi Province as "Ratchaburi is the town of dragon-jar".

The jars are all local made products and very famous for their unique design of dragon painted. The jars are for keeping the rain water for daily using since the ancient time, but nowadays some people buy them for home decorations. The design of the dragon jar is also painted on many things like; plant pots, vases and souvenirs which are very popular; it looks antique and last long.

The distance from Bangkok to the old and beautiful floating market is approximately 100 kms by heading to the west of Bangkok. Ratchaburi is close to Kanchanaburi, Nakorn Pathom, Samutsakorn, Samutsongkram, Petchaburi and some part of Myanmar at the west.

The main river pass through the center of the province is The Mae Klong River which flows from Kanchanaburi to the Gulf of Thailand in Samutsongkram Province.

Figure 163 Damnoensaduak, Ratchaburi

Damnoensaduak Floating Market

Figure 164 Vendors for food and desserts sold in canal at Damnoensaduak

❑ This floating market was named after Damnoensaduak Canal which was a man-made canal in 1904, in the reign of King Rama V.

❏   The canal is now the center for all vendors sell their own agricultural products and some handicrafts.

This canal was dug from the order of King Rama IV, the purpose was for connecting to Mae Klong and Tha Chin Rivers for the conveniences of trade and transportation. It was dug for about 2 years, finished in the reign of King Rama 5[th.]

Damnoensaduak Canal was made in straight line of 32 kms. long and become the longest canal in Thailand. There are about 200 canals separated from it.

Most of the local people earn their livings by gardening. Coconut Juice is very sweet and well known as well as the natural sugar palm fresh juice and sugar cake. All vendors are friendly and kind.

At Damnoensaduak Floating Market

❏   Must try riding Sampan Boat; a small boat as a transport in this area, all the locals here have this kind of boat at least one boat for traveling.

I remembered the event which shocked me when my guest; a very large sized man fell into the canal when he stepped on a small boat and the boat turned upside down in the canal right away. He finally could get in the boat and; with a sense of humor, he asked if I would like to join this small boat tour with him; "I like to but I really can not swim!"

What a surprise! He could row the boat very expertly among the vendors and went into the Tha Chin River a while. I was worried about safety but he enjoyed the trip very much. I was really happy whenever my guests did what they loved to do or tried things they should do once in a lifetime here. But I would always consider "safety first" for my clients during touring with me. He's a very kind man and had much sense of humors all the time tours in Thailand with me.

❏ You can also come to the center of the market by land and rent a speed boat for tour around the canal. (in case coming from Kanchanaburi or other provinces nearby) The good time for seeing the beautiful view of plenty of boats is between 8.00-13.00 daily.

❏ Visit the National Museum in Ratchaburi; it's the old city hall with pink color buildings, located at the center of the province in the past, which is the museum nowadays.

❏ Visit The Elephant Village.

Figure 165 The Smoke of Bats at Khao Chong Pran, Ratchaburi

❑ Discover Khao Chong Pran or Bat Cave. During sunset, millions of bats flying into the sky like a black smoke from the mountain. It's amazing there!

❑ Explore Khao Ngu Stone Park; it's away from Ratchaburi town about 8 kilometers, you can hike to many beautiful caves, but watch out the big group of monkeys around here.

Khao Ngu Stone Park

Figure 166 Khao Ngu Stone Park, Ratchaburi

PETCHABURI

Figure 167 Khao Wang, Petchaburi

❑ Petchaburi is a nice province with many attractions and it's where Cha-Am Beach located. It's one of the nearest beaches to Bangkok, located at the southwest of Thailand and close to Hua Hin.

- The former name of Petchaburi was "Phra Nakhon Khiri" or known as **"Khao Wang"**; The Historical Palace with Museum on the hill nowadays. When you reach Petchaburi, you can notice a temple on a hill seen from very far.

- It's about 130 kilometers from Bangkok, nearby provinces are; Ratchaburi, Samutsongkram and Prachuapkhirikhan. The west of the province borders Myanmar.
- This seaside province is mostly mountainous and forest areas with many wildlife. The famous and popular park for adventurers is **Kaeng Kra Chan National Park**. It's the largest national park in Thailand and was declared as UNESCO Natural World Heritage in 2021.

Transportation:

Car, Buses (at the Southern Bus Terminal), Buses at Suwannaphum Airport (**Bus to Hua Hin at 1st floor**)

Rail: stop at Cha Am or Petchaburi Station.

If you choose to stay in Hua Hin, you can also visit Petchaburi for a day tour. Or if you stay at Cha Am Beach, you can visit Hua Hin also.

Figure 168 Khaeng Krachan Dam

Figure 169 Phranakon Khiri, Khao Luang Cave, Prang Dang

❑ **Explore the areas of Phra Nakhon Khiri, The Royal Palace and Wat Phra Kaew Noi :**

❑ **The Sala Thasana Nakkhataroek**; the pavilion for the king's watching the festivals and cultural show, located at the hillside. Admire

❑ **Phra Prang Daeng**; the red color stupa, "Daeng" means "Red", it's a corncob-shaped stupa, with the seat for Buddha Statue found inside.

- **Wat Phra Kaew Noi Chapel**; a small ordination hall made of marbles and some colored tiles with triangle gable decorated with a beautiful Thai Style Patterns. There are two pavilions nearby the temple.
- **Hor Jatuwate Paritpath**; a pavilion for religious ceremony.
- **Phra Suttha Sala Chedi**; a small pagoda of 9 meter high is put on a high base, contains Buddha's Relic, located behind the ordination hall of the temple.
- **The Bell Tower** in front of the hall.
- Walk along to the small hill at the east and see the group of old pavilions and the royal garage.
- **Ratchawanlapakan**; a building for the king's courtiers, police and followers.
- **Sala Yen Jai**; a building for civil servants, separated on the slope of the hill.
- **Sala Dan Klang**; the building of the head-checkpoint and the Horse Stable.
- **Sala Luk Khun**; a jury station.
- **Sala Dan Na**; the resting area for the king's police.
- **The Watchara Phiban Fortress.**
- **Santhakarn Sathan Throne Hall**; a royal villa with a big building and a stage in front of the pavilion.
- **The Royal Pantry and the Royal Kitchen.**
- Tim Dab Ongkarak; a resting place for the royal guards.
- **Petch Poom Pai Rot Throne Hall;** the biggest throne hall in the palace and **Pramot Mahai Sawan Throne Hall.**
- **Phra Tinang Ratcha Dhamma Sapa Throne Hall.**
- **Phra Tinang Watechayan Wichien Prasart Throne Hall;** the building with Prangs and kept a bronze statue of King Rama IV inside.

- **Hor Chatchawan Wiengchai**; a dome-shaped on the top roof with lanterns hanging inside; the lights from this dome can be seen from the sea which look as if it's a lighthouse for the fishermen. There is a flag-post in front of the building.
- **Sala Dan Lang;** a resting place for checkers.

Figure 170 The Dome Building at Phranakon Khiri, Petchaburi

☐ Discover **Khao Luang Cave which is only** 5 kilometers from **Khao Wang the Palace. If you arrive** during 9.30-10.30 am., you will see the lights shone from the holes like, the big spotlight on the cave floor.

☐ There are many old temples with beautiful Buddhist Art in craftsmanship of ancient architectures and sculptures in Petchaburi Town such as:

- The unique design of Buddhist Art at **Wat Khoy**, where some of Buddha's relic kept on the top of the big Buddha Statues situated inside the hall.
- The beautiful and unique architecture of 5 Pagodas at **Wat Mahathat Voraviharn.**
- **Wat Kho Keaw Suttharam;** known as one of the oldest temple in Petchaburi, is full of many ancient buildings.
- **Wat Yai Suwannaram; is only a** kilometer from the city hall. The mural paintings here are over 300 years old.
- **Wat Tham Khao Yoi;** the cave nearby the main road, it's where King Rama IV practiced meditation during his monkhood.
- **Wat Kuti near Khoa Yoi;** the beautiful craftsmanship of The Ordination Hall built from carved teak wood.
- ❏ Enjoy walking around the local community market in Petchaburi such as, street of art and food, home of several desserts; you must try **Mor Kaeng,** the famous dessert or local custard cake made from eggs and taro or pumpkin mixed with natural brown sugar palm tree and coconut milk. The tourists who pass by Petchaburi mostly get Mor Keang as the best souvenirs to friends and family, it can be kept in refrigerator for a week. Many of the local desserts are found nearby the Petchaburi River.

Khanom Mor Kaeng

- ❑ Admire the beautiful buildings of European architecture Style at **Ban Puen Palace;** it's the palace built in the reign of King Rama 5th which was a palace used during rainy season.
- ❑ Enjoy the beach at **Had Chao Sam Ran**, it's the beach of old time and it's the peaceful beach, good for relaxing.
- ❑ Explore the mangrove forest at **Laem Pak Bear of Ban Laem** and watch the various kinds of birds. The wooden bridge of 850 meter long is nice here.
- ❑ Walk along **The Cha Am Beach; it's** away from Hua Hin Beach for about 20 kilometers. You can find many nice beach resorts and hotels with some fresh seafood restaurants here.

Figure 171 Cha Am, Petchaburi

- ❑ Explore **Keang Krachan National Park;** it was named to be **UNESCO Natural World Heritage Site** on July 26, 2021, the popular national park for camping. The park is located near the dam and it's well known for watching the birds and magnificent views of misty mountains in the early morning.

□   If you visit the park in April-June, you will discover the swarm of butterflies at Ban Krang camp; part of Keang Krachan National Park. This amazing nature happens once a year, and it's like, a festival for butterflies. They all come for food at salt lick area at **8.00-14.00.**

❑ Before you enter Hua Hin, you will see the beautiful Summer Palace, **Ma-ruk-ka-thai-ya-wan; it's** located between Cha Am and Hua Hin Beach. It's built in 1923 in the reign of King Rama VI. The palace is the two-storey wooden pavilion with halls connecting each other joined by pathways and a long corridor leading to the sea.

Figure 172 Ma Ruek Kha Tai Ya Wan Palace

Figure 173 The Royal Pavilion at Hua Hin Train Station

PRACHUP KHIRI KHUN

Prachup Khiri Khun is called "City of The Three Bays"; Noi Bay, Prachub Bay and Manao Bay are in the areas of this province. It's the western province of Thailand and about 250 kilometers from Bangkok.

Its neighboring provinces are; Petchaburi to the north, Chumporn to the south and borders Myanmar to the west. This province is at the narrowest part of Thailand which heading to the Southern Region. The famous place belongs to this province is Hua Hin; a district which is popular as the old fashioned resort town.

TRANSPORT: RAIL: stop at; Hua Hin, Nong Kae, Khao Tao, Suan Son, Pranburi, Kan Kradai, and Prachuapkhirikhan Stations. You choose where to go and should experience the Thai train. **Buses** are available at the airport for Hua Hin. If you prefer the private transport; please go to Tour Service or taxi, but **air planes or Ferry boats** can be done from Pattaya.

Figure 174 Hua Hin

Figure 175 Hua Hin Night Market

❑ Night Market or "Talad Toa Loong" of Hua Hin is the first place to enjoy in the evening when you get in Hua Hin Town. It's where there are plenty of restaurants and vendors by the pathways selling all kinds of delicious food and souvenirs from 5 pm till midnight or dawn. If you reach Hua Hin, you may need a motorbike for roaming around, like going to the beaches and along the suburbs. Don't forget to ride "Ma Krab" or a small horse along the beach.

❑ **See "Luang Por Thoud";** a large statue of sacred monk which is well respected among Thai, situated at **Wat Huay Mongkol.** It's 14 kilometers from Hua Hin downtown. The temple is full of the beautiful scenery and Buddhist Arts with nature surroundings.

❑ **Catch a glimpse of the first rays over Hua Hin Town at Khao Hin Lek Fai;** 3 kilometers from downtown, the best viewpoints for the entire town of Hua Hin. (Can also go during sunset but it's crowded.)

- ❏ **Explore Pa La U** Waterfall; drive about 65 kilometers from Hua Hin and trek in the jungles. You should walk in the cold waterfall for refreshing. The waterfall is in the area of Kaeng Kra Chan National Park.
- ❏ Get **splashed at Vana Nava Water Park**; the water jungle, include rides, slides and many activities.
- ❏ Spend hours **thrilling wakeboarding** at Black Mountain Wake Park near Hua Hin Town.
- ❏ **Enjoy the Seenspace Hua Hin,** the community mall on the beach.
- ❏ Get a glimpse of souvenirs and local goods at **Cicada Market; a night market** at Suansri in front of Hyatt Regency Hotel in Hua Hin downtown. There are some dancing shows here.

Figure 176 Khao Tao Village and the temple

- Visit **Khao Tao Fabrics Fine Hand Woven and Cotton Fabric**; a project from The Royal Project of The King Rama 9th , for helping local people to have a career as the handmade producers in a fine unique designed fabrics. It becomes international well known called "Pha Khao Mah" nowadays.
- Climb the top of **Khao Takiap** and see the best viewpoint of beautiful sea and Hua Hin Beaches. Wat Khao Takiep is at the hilltop. You can ride a pick-up bus from downtown here.

Figure 177 Khao Takiep

❏ See **the huge Standing Buddha at the cliff** of Khao Takiap Hill, and the place is the landmark for Khao Takiep. Many bungalows and resort hotels are around in this peaceful beach.

❏ From Khao Takiep; you will see another beach nearby which is clean and nice for swimming in the sea which is called **Suan Son Beach; "Son" means "Pine Tree", "Suan" means "Garden", this** white sand beach is full of many pine trees range by the beach. It's located between Khoa Takiap amd Khao Tao. Stay overnight here is great!

Figure 178Suan Son Beach

❏ The Pavilion in Lake at Khao Tao Water Reservoir for His Majesty King Bhumipol. He initiated The Project of fresh water for villagers in Khao Tao Village; a fishermen village. **Khao Tao** is a fisherman Village Town, a nice place for visiting. You can walk from Suan Son Beach for a nice seafood restaurant by the beach here. Walk around to the lake to admire the beautiful Pavilion in the lake which is for a memorial of His Majesty King Bhumibol. There's a hill nearby, the location of **Wat Khao Tao, a** small temple with a very nice viewpoint of the sea.

Figure 179 The Pavilion in the lake at Kao Tao and the beach

Figure 180 Khao Kalok, Pranburi

PRANBURI

Pranburi is a district which is next to Hua Hin. There are many attractions in this area and one of tourists' choices to stay and relax. The road from Khao Tao passes through tourist attractions in Pranburi.

❏ Visit the beaches **at Pak Nam Pran**, an old fisherman village town in **Pranbur**i District. The place is a peaceful place and can see a beautiful sunrise here.

❏ Pranburi District has many nice places for looking around such as, **Sirinart Rajini Ecosystem Learning Center; a** mangrove forest and natural surroundings.

Don't forget to taste a spicy **fresh seafood** from the fishermen's restaurant at **Pak Nam Pran**.

- ❑ Explore the beaches from Pak Nam Pran to **Khao Kalok or "Skull Hill"** (Kalok means skull) and enjoy the white sand beach which lied 10 kilometers long and enter **The Thao KO SA Forest Park.**

- ❑ Explore **Khao Sam Roi Yot National Park;** the marine park in Thailand, 60 kilometers from Hua Hin to the south. The park includes Thailand's largest fresh water marsh. "Sam Roi Yot" means "300 peaks" which are seen in this highland of the mountainous areas. If you have time, you must visit here. It's a wonderful adventure for trailing and exploring.

- ❑ Hike 500 meters to the viewpoint at **Khao Daeng**, getting panorama view of Pranburi Beach and limestone mountain range. (Wear rubber shoes for hiking the hill and water for drink)

Figure 181 The view of Sam Roi Yod Mountain

❏ Admire the blooming Lotus at the **Lotus Lake or Bueng Bua** of the park, the best time is in October-April.

❏ **Sam Phraya Beach,** with soft white sand and pine trees, where. you can pitch a tent at the beach.

❏ Explore and hike to **Phraya Nakhon** Cave, a large cave where the kings visited. You can rent a boat and climb up the mountain about 430 meters or 1400 feet to reach the cave. Although the weather is hot but It's worth hiking to this beautiful cave.

Figure 182 The Khuha Kharuehart Pavilion, Phayanakon Cave

- ❏ Discover **The Khuha Kharuehat Pavilion**, a historic site built for The King Rama V since 1890, a symbol of PrachuapKhiri Khan Province, located inside the Phraya Nakorn Cave. The inside cave is like a large parlor.

- ❏ Explore more of **Keaw Cave and Sai Cave** nearby.

- ❏ Snorkeling under the clear ocean water at **Koh Jan and Koh Tai Sea** in the area of **Vanakorn National Park** to see a beautiful corals and fishes.

- ❏ **Discover Koh Talu**, a beautiful and amazed island with crystal clear ocean water, great for snorkeling.

- ❏ **Hike at Lom Muak Hill;** 300 meter high for a panorama view of the three bays belong to Prachuap Khiri Khan Province. The bays are Noi Bay, Prachuap Bay and Manao Bay. (Please check the schedule for hiking the hill.)

Figure 183 Prchub Bay

☐ Escape to **Prachuap Bay**; lies off Prachuap Khiri Khan town about 8 kilometers, and enjoy walking around this bayside for a fabulous views of many small islands..

☐ **Must visit!** The absolute beautiful architecture of the Compound of Nine Pagodas and the huge stunning Buddha Statue in sitting position facing the seaside is at **Wat Tang Sai,** a temple which located nearby the seashore at **Ban Grood.**

☐ Admire the image of The Buddha Statue in reclining position built in **the Cave of Noi Bay Temple** or Wat Ao Noi; the place where you can see a beautiful Ordination Hall made of teak wood and decorated with the two giant Naka Heads at the entrance of the temple.

Figure 184 Khao Chong Krajok, Prachub

❑ Amazed the views at the hilltop **of Khao Chong Krachok in town; here is called "The Monkey Mountain", you have to** climb for 395 steps for viewing the ocean view. Watch out the monkeys!

AO PRACHUP

Figure 185 Kuiburi National Park, Prachup Khiri khan

❑ **Watching the wild elephants at Kui Buri National Park**; the best wild elephant watching spot in Thailand. The park is evergreen rain forests full of wildlife such as, elephants, gaurs and others. It's in Kui Buri District of Prachuap Khiri Khan Province.

Figure 186 Manao Bay

❑ **Swim in Manao Bay**, 5 kilometers south of Prachuap town, a beautiful curved bay which is one of popular destinations among tourists.

❑ Splash clear ocean water and relax at a peaceful bay. It's less crowded at **Ao Bo Thonglang, the bay** with the half -circle shape beach; when it's low, tide, a small island appear.

❑ Discover the **Sing Khon Pass**, the Checkpoint to Myanmar, located at the narrowest part of Thailand in Prachuap. Khiri Khan Province.

❑ Check in a small hotel at the bay town and relax.

Figure 187 Prachup Town

CHACHOENGSAO

Figure 188 Luang Por Sothon

❏ Chachoengsao Province is connected to Bangkok at the east side and known as an agricultural hub of central region. The main river is called Bang Pakong River runs the length of this province. Most people have settled their homes by the river since The Ayutthaya Period.
It borders; Pathumthani, Nakornnayok, Prachinburi, Sa Kaew, Chantaburi, Chonburi and Samutprakarn.

Travelling to Chachoengsao is easy from the airport, takes an hour to its downtown. It's about 80 kilometers from Bangkok.

The province is famous among Thai Buddhists for worshipping Luang Por Sothon; one of the most sacred Buddha Statue in Thailand and the landmark of Cha Choeng Sao Province.

❑ **Wat Sothon Wararam Worawihan** or the former name called "Wat Hong" in the municipal area of Chachoengsao Province. This temple was built in the late Ayutthaya period and located along the Bang Pakong River. The temple has a large construction of Phra Viharn for housing the statue of **"Luang Por Sothon",** one of the most important and sacred Buddha statue in Thailand.

• The statue was built in sitting position of meditation attitude. Almost everyday, the pavilion is crowded with the Thai Buddhists; they come to pay respect, putting gold leaves on the image and wish for good luck.

❑ Discover and **"The Ordination Hall and Pagoda in the Sea"** at Wat Hong Thong, on the edge of the Gulf of Thailand and enjoy the seaview from the top of the Pagoda.

❑ **Hire a boat** at Wat Sothorn Pier for looking around local living on both sides of the banks of Bangpakong River.

The trip is about 25 kms along the river or 3 hours ride. You can see a typical Thai local living in the old days exists here.

- ❑ Discover "Talat Klong Suan"; the amazing market where the two provinces, Chachoengsao and Samutprakarn Provinces connect each other just only by crossing the canal which is only a small bridge. You don't even know where you are; Chachoengsao or Samutprakan!
- • It's the market for enjoying walking and eating typical Thai food from the local Thai community of old style. Some of the rarely old Thai desserts are found here.
- ❑ Discover **"Talat Ban Mai"** or "100 year Market". It's the market of variety of good food, Thai snacks and local souvenirs.
- ❑ If you have time, you can visit a temple around here for admiring the beautiful Ordination Hall made from Stainless steel at **Wat Hua Suan.**

Figure 189 The light decorations at Wat Sothon

PRACHINBURI

Figure 190 Wat Chaeng, Prachinburi

- ❑ Prachinburi is the province of a long historical background and a very large province. The two provinces; Nakornnayok and Sa Keaw were districts belong to this province before, but they were separated to be the provinces later.
- • Prachinburi is the important province for economic of the east because there are many foreign investments and industrial estates are established within the province.

- The province areas are mostly covered with mountains Nakornratchasima, Chachoengsao, Sa Keaw and Nakornnayok.
- Transportation:
- By cars/taxi, By Bus; from the Northern Bus Terminal near Jatujak Park, By Rail; it takes about 4 hours and get off at Prachinburi or Kabinburi Stations.

Figure 191 Wat Keaw Phijit, Prachinburi

❑ If we visit any province in Thailand, we usually look for the landmark of the town and most of them are the beautiful temples. **Wat Keaw Phijit** is the landmark of Prachinburi where the ordination hall is stunning and beautiful interior decorations of mural paintings and the principal Buddha image. The temple is only 2 kilometers from downtown.

❑ Wat Chaeng is in Prachinburi town, close to Wat Keaw Phijit. See the stunning pagoda of Buddha's Relic at the middle of lake; the pagoda is the same style of Phrathart Phanom Pagoda, the famous and important pagoda in Nakonpanom, at the northeastern of Thailand.

- ❑ **Wat Ton Pho Srimahapoat is where** the oldest Pho Tree in Thailand which is a sacred site for local people in Prachinburi. The temple is about 22 kilometers from downtown.
- ❑ Don't forget to visit **The Chao Phraya Apaipubeth Museum**, the collections of Herbal Plants Research Books and Traditional Thai Medical Center, includes products and services; herbs, massages and spa, 2.5 kilometers from town.
- ❑ Admire the beautiful Buddha image; in sitting position with 7 head-Naka, the statue is 14.9 meter wide and 34 meter long situated about 3 kilometers from Jakkapong Water Reservior; the lake is popular for kayaking, bicycling and camping. If you pass by here, you will enjoy a nice view and a peaceful place.
- ❑ Discover the biggest museum of lamps in Asia; called **Yoo Suk Suwan Museum** at Pachantakam District.

Figure 192 Fireflies or Hing Hoi at Prachinburi

If you stay overnight in Prachinburi, you may choose a resort where you can see the fabulous Ngon Nak Flowers fields which look like a lavender fields. It's nice to see during 7.00am-3.00pm.

❑ Discover the amazing **Fireflies** Land at Promyothi Military Camp during June-July at 6.30-8.30 pm. The land is lighted from million of fireflies like, stars shone all over the land.

❑ Adventure at **Tab Lan National Park**; 32 kilometers from downtown where is a popular place for camping and g the nature trails in the park. The park areas cover two provinces; Prachinburi andenjoyin Nakorn Ratcha Sima.

❑ The famous for rapids rafting in Thailand in rainy season is at **Keang Hin Ploeng, for enjoying** the one hour rafting in July-November. It's in Khao Yai National Park areas

Figure 193 Gnon nak Flower Bloom Nov-Dec in Prachinburi

KHAO YAI NATIONAL PARK

❑ Khao Yai National Park is the park cover many provinces include Prachinburi area. You can hike at Prachinburi (recommend with local guide) for about 4 kilometers to see a very beautiful waterfall; **Hell E Arm** Waterfall and **Tad Hin Yao Waterfall.** You must contact the Office of the park for hiking here.

❏ Khao Yai is also situated in the area of Nakonratchasima Province; the gate to Isan or the northeastern region where you can explore many places besides; Khao Yai. Mostly people come to Khao Yai here for seeing the wild elephants in the forests; sometimes they lie on the road and harm the tourists.

*Travelling to Khao Yai is easy from the Suwannaphum Airport; by taxi or rent a car to go there takes only 2 hours; if you would like to get away from city for seeing the rural areas, you must come to Khao Yai and Wang Nam Kheiw. You will enjoy the nature and local living along the way with a good climate. You can check in somewhere at one of the resorts or hotels for a night. It's quiet near to Pak Chong; a district of Nakon ratchasima where you get fresh air and picturesque small town.

Wang Nam Kheiw District also is one of the tourists' destinations in Nakonratchasima for ozone and watching the gaurs closely at Khao Phang Ma Non-Hunting Area; the top hit Gaur point for tourists in cool season.

Farmstays, Homestays and resorts are fully booked during this cool season; November-February. You must experience here and enjoy Khao Yai, Wang Nam Khiew and Pak Chong; one of the top bucket lists Thailand.

Figure 194 Guars at Khao Phaeng Ma

Figure 195 Khao Yai

- ❑ **Boat for hire** along Prachinburi River about 2 hours for visiting many places. The boat trip in Thailand is the best part of the tour for seeing the local living along the bank of the river. You should not miss the boat trip.
- ❑ **Dinosaur Garden is an** entertainment for kids and family.
- ❑ **Dadsada Gallery is a gallery for** the collections of flowers in season and feel fresh anytime you visit here.
- ❑ **Prachinburi National Museum.**

❑ **The Verona Tab Lan is a community mall and entertainment areas which came from** the owner's inspiration of Verona City in Italy. The architecture is mimicking of its atmosphere and some buildings. There are hundred shops around with some restaurants etc.

Figure 196 Namtok Takro and Namtok Saladdi, Khao Yai National Park, Prachinburi

SA KEAW

❑ Sa Keaw was announced as the province in 1993, a large district separated from Prachinburi. This province was a Refugee Camp in 1979 and closed in 1989.

The province areas are parts of the Thai-Cambodia border at the east. The provincial land was a part of border lines, known as the largest land mine field in the world.

❑ Sa Keaw is about 200 kilometers from Bangkok. Normally; it's a province where people cross the border at the gate to Cambodia. You will see lots of temples in this province built in Cambodian Style. The landmark of Sa Kaeo is the largest Khmer Temple in Thailand called The **Sadok Kok Thom Khmer Temple**; Sadok Kok Thom is a Khmer language means "It is cluttered with Reeds".

• It's located in Khok Sung District, about 34 kilometers from the border of Aranyapratet District. The temple architecture is similar to Angkor Wat in Cambodia but its size is smaller.

It was declared as the national historical park in 2017 and become a popular tourist attraction in Sa Keaw Province.

Figure 197 Sadok Kok Thom Temple, Sa Kaew

Sadok Kok Thom Historical Park

❑ See the **Barai**; a rectangle-shaped water reservoir, away from the Temple about 175 meters.

❑ See the **Corridor Insulation**; the floor was made of laterite and decorated with 86 carved stone columns in square shapes along the pathway to Sadok Kok Thom Temple.

❑ Admire **The Arched Entrance and Defensive Wall**; made of laterite in rectangle-shaped of wall layout.

❑ See **The Cloister** building which was made of laterite and sandstone, left with damaged roof but some of carvings on pediments and lintels still appear.

❏ See **the U-Shaped Pool**; around the Temple.

The main sacred temple was stunning from its unique architectural Shrine. It's the most important Prang built in 5-tier from the peak with carvings and a large construction made of sandstone and a double-layer square base made of laterite. The gate was found decorated with beautiful columns and having stairways to the main Prang. There are short columns around the main temple.

❏ The Bannalai or the cloister areas was found with laterite courtyard with Naka (Naka is a mythical serpent related to Buddhism) on the roofs around the main temple.

❏ Aranya Prathet District is an important town for trade and transportation borders Cambodia at the east. The road here is to Siem Reap, the nearest town to Angkor Wat.

• I came to this district in 1989 when the road was still narrow and secluded. The buildings in those days were the old wooden style. The gate to Cambodia was not opened yet; it's opened in 1998. The district looked very impressive with many old buildings and temples, but it's still dangerous zone.

❏ At the present, the crowded area of Sa Keaw is in Aranyaprathet District, or called by Thai as "Aran", where many illegal activities like; gambling and car-stolen from Thailand to Cambodia passed this Aran boundary. If you prefer to go to Cambodia by road, it's the most popular by here.

❏ Explore **Lalu**; a natural phenomenon from the rainwater caused the soil land erosion making the hard, solid soil become rock formations in different shapes naturally, called as one of Thailand's Canyon, located at Ta Phraya District; a district borders Cambodia at the east.

Figure 198 Lalu, Sa Kaew

- ❑ **Prasart Khao Noi Si Chomphu was** assumed that its architecture influenced by Hinduism beliefs from 12th Century, located in Aranyapratet District, away from the border 1 kilometer.
- ❑ **Pang Sida National Park** is one of popular park for camping and best known for Namtok Pang Sida; a single Waterfall 8 meter high to a large basin at the ground. Camping and nature trails in this park are the season for watching butterflies in June-July. The fresh water crocodiles found at a large lake, away from the park about 5 kilometers, is the only one left in Thailand.
- ❑ Discover a beautiful viewpoint and a nice atmosphere at **Pha Deang**, of **Ta Phraya National Park;** covering two provinces area of Sa Kaeo and Buriram which border Cambodia.
- ❑ Visit **Rong Kluea Market;** or called Klong Luek Market in Aranyapratet District near the checkpoint of the boundary, having about 1300 stores in the large market selling variety of goods from mostly Cambodia.

Figure 199 Chonburi, Sattaheep, Toey Ngam Beach

CHONBURI

- Chonburi Province is not known as much as "Pattaya City". Their locations are in the same area of Chonburi; a province at the east coast of Thailand where it's the location of Laem Chabang Sea Port; a very important sea port of the east. It's an old town where ancient items was found and assumed that, it's the land of pre-historic community lived. It's about 80 kilometers from Bangkok and about 40 kilometers from Pattaya.
- The Neighboring provinces are Chachoengsao, Rayong, Chanthaburi and the Gulf of Thailand.

- Travelling to Chonburi is normally by car/taxi (takes about 1 hour from the airport, by rail; get off at Chonburi City, by bus; at the Suwannaphum Airport, and by plane to U-Tapao Airport.

Figure 200 Khao Chee Chan, Chonburi

- **Khao Chi Chan** is where The Laser Buddha Mountain image on the cliff built to honor His Majesty King Bhumibol on the occasion of his Golden Jubilee. The place is at Na Chom Thian in Sattaheep district, of Chonburi Province.
- ❑ **Sattaheep** District is the Thai Naval Base location in Chonburi Province. It's about 80 kilometers from Chonburi and 30 Kilometers from Pattaya.
- ❑ There are many tourist attractions like, beautiful islands in Sattaheep Bay. If you would like to relax in a peaceful place and swim in a crystal clear water then stay here because it's not so far from U-Tapao Airport.

❑ Sattaheep Beaches are where there are many interesting places and sea sports like, scuba diving, snorkeling, kayaking, banana boat from these popular islands and beaches such as,

❑ **Ko Kham**; a beautiful island with coral range, nice for snorkeling. You can take a boat to the island at Khao Ma Jor Pier.

❑ **Ko Samaesan** is Thai Island and Sea Nature History Museum. It's nice for diving. Explore many beaches and interesting places in Sattaheep such as;

   ❑ Bang Saleh Boathouse.

   ❑ Diving Points at Sattaheep;

   ❑ Sai Keaw Beach,

   ❑ Toey Ngam Beach,

   ❑ Kret Keaw Beach,

   ❑ Nang Rong Beach,

   ❑ Nang Rum Beach,

   ❑ Nam Sai Beach,

   ❑ Bang Sa leh Beach,

   ❑ Sau Beach,

   ❑ Sattaheep Beach,

   ❑ Dong Tan Bay,

   ❑ Ban Ampher Beach,

   ❑ Admire the beautiful viewpoint at Luang Por Dam Temple,

   ❑ Discover HTMS Chakri Naruebet; this ship is the smallest functioning aircraft carrier in the world.

❑ Explore **Nong Nooch Garden Pattaya**; the large tropical garden; about 1700 rais, many botanical gardens and tourist attractions located in Sattaheep District.

❑ Splash and slide into The Columbia Pictures Aquaverse; the Theme Park in Na Jomtien.

- ❏ Admire the great art at Art in Paradise Pattaya; the art gallery with amazing 3D arts and enjoy picturing yourself here.
- ❏ Discover The Sriracha Tiger Zoo; the zoo is on the way to Pattaya, about 97 kilometers from Bangkok, full of tigers and crocodiles.
- ❏ Visit Khao Kheow Open Zoo of about 2000 acres, contains many kinds of animals from various species. It's in Sriracha District.
- ❏ Visit **Bangsean Beach**; the popular beach among Thai tourists where there are many nice seafood restaurants and attractions nearby for tours. You still see some local living at the local market near Bangsean.

Figure 201 Pattaya, Koh Lan, The Sanctuary of Truth

Figure 202 Pattaya City

PATTAYA CITY

❏ Pattaya City is in Banglamung District of Chonburi but it's considered as special town where the city is self governing municipal area covers the north, center, south Pattaya Beaches and Jom Tien Beach. It's about 120 kilometers from Bangkok to the east coastal areas of the Gulf of Thailand. You can easily find everything in Pattaya City.

- ❑ Ride the boat to **Ko Lan;** the Coral Island, and experience one night camping in this small island; it's off the coast of Pattaya, in the Gulf of Thailand with clear water and nice atmosphere. Try one of water sport activities.
- ❑ Walk along the long beach at **Jomtien** Community; it's clean and quiet beach, enjoy watching the sunset there.
- ❑ Explore the walking street and red-light district in the Pattaya City after sunset.
- ❑ Discover the **cabaret shows**; a wonderful entertainment at the Pattaya walking street.
- ❑ Admire the beautiful artwork of The Sanctuary of Truth or **Prasart Satchatham**; wood carving buildings of ancient Thai architecture.
- ❑ Visit Suan Suea or Tiger Park Pattaya at Banglamoong.
- ❑ Enjoy the Sampan Boat trip for looking around at **The Four -Region Floating Market**; the market modeled of traditional Thai life styles from the four regions; like, culture shows, houses, shops, food and local souvenirs.

RAYONG

☐ Rayong is the province connected to Pattaya City. Most of the tourists who stay in Pattaya visit Rayong for changing climate and see some fascinating beaches and scenery at Ko Samet, before moving to explore Chanthaburi and Trat Provinces.

• Although the province is the main center for industrial estates; chemical and auto industries, but there are many nice beaches, places and nature for visiting.

- It's about 180 kilometers from Bangkok by car; passing through the motorway and see the sign of Rayong Province. It's only 60 kms from Pattaya City.
- In the past, Rayong was the base where King Taksin (of Thonburi Period); during that time he was the leader who hit the breakout of Burmese Army during the Fall of Ayutthaya, assembled the soldiers in Rayong before moving to settle the army in Chanthaburi Province and finally restored a fallen state to be independent from Burma in 1767 and established Thonburi (the other side of The Chao Phraya River bank opposite Bangkok) to be the capital in his period.

Figure 203 Suan Sr Muan Rayong City Park

❑ **Wat Lum Mahachai Chumpon** was the base and where The King Taksin Shrine situated for remind the Thai people of hishis success from fighting against the Burmese Army and restored the independence to the nation.

❑ Discover Pla Beach; the first beach next to Chonburi Province located at Banchang District which is near the U-Tapao airport.

❑ Swim at Phayoon Beach and enjoy the places around like, Luang Tier Phayoon Shrine Dragon Bridge.

❑ Relax a while at Nam Rin Beach.

❑ Admire Phra Chedi Klang Nam; a pagoda nearby Rayong River in the center of Rayong town and visit the Mangrove Forest Learning Center nearby.

❑ Swim in the beautiful clear sea water at **Mae Rum Poeng Beach**; the popular beach among tourists and this place is full of seafood restaurants.

❑ Visit Rayong Aquarium and educational exhibits on the fishing industry.

❑ Trail at Khap Laem Ya National park. It's a nice view and good for camping.

❑ Visit **Laem Jaroen Beach**; the nearest beach to Rayong downtown, the place is famous for fish sauce production. This beach is also famous for seafood restaurants.

❑ **Saeng Chan Beach** is nearby town.

❑ Ban Pe Pier is the pier where you can ride the boat to **Ko Samet (See Explore 29 Islands)** and look around. The island is the fisherman market where tourists buy local products.

• Explore Ko Samet; a white sand beaches with clear water and beautiful coral reefs and don't forget to explore; Ao Prao, Laem Toei and Sai Keaw Beach

❑ Visit HTMS Prasae Memorial; a ship museum and walk around the areas.

❑ Discover Tung Prong Thong or the Golden Meadow; by walking through the dense mangrove forests along boardwalk trails or riding a boat to enjoy the scenery here.

❑ See **Sunthorn Phu Monument**; a statue of famous Thai Poet of **"Phra Apaimanee"** Literature. The sculptures of the characters of this love story in the poem are situated nearby.

❑ Ride the boat at Laem Tan Pier at Ao Kai in Klang District to explore the group of **Man Islands**; Ko Man Nok, Ko Man Klang and Ko Man Nai, the three islands with white sand beaches and crystal clear water. The sea turtles at The Turtle Nursery Center are in Ko Man Nai. You can swim and kayak at Ko Man Nok and Ko Man Klang.

Adventure in the jungle at **Khao Chamao – Khao Wong National Park for;** it's famous for a beautiful 8- tier waterfall from the peak of Chamao Mountain flow for 3 kms downward, you should hike and see fish in each layer of waterfall. After Rayong Province, you can travel a little bit distance for Chanthaburi. It's not only famous for gem mines, but also it's an old town full of attractions in the east.

Figure 204 Chanthaburi, Noen Nang Phaya View Point

CHANTHABURI

❑ Chanthaburi is the province next to Rayong. It's the center of gem mines and the land of fruits. The neighboring provinces are; Chachoengsao and Sa Keaw at the north, Trat and Cambodia at the east, Chonburi and Rayong at the west and The Gulf of Thailand at south.

• The distance from Bangkok to Chanthaburi is about 240 kms. The highest mountain of the east region in Thailand is Khao Soy dao located in this province. It's about 1,675 meter ASL.

- Chanthaburi was one of the important provinces, an abundant land for food in the history. King Taksin chose here as the base for assemble the soldiers to fight against Burmese Army and finally restored independence to Thailand or Siam that time.

Chanthaburi

- Traveling to Chanthaburi from Bangkok is by private car, taxi, buses at the Aekamai Bus Terminal; this terminal is for all provinces in the east region, you can go by BTS; at Aekamai Station.

- ❏ Discover the landmark of Chanthaburi at Nearn Nang Phraya Viewpoint where you can see the curve of the road near the beaches.
- ❏ Discover the old Pagoda of more than 200 years old situated in the sea. You can walk 50 meters on the wooden bridge built by villagers there to see.
- ❏ Explore the Learning Center for Mangrove Forest at Ao Koong Kraben and see Aquarium inside the Learning Center.
- ❏ **Laem Sadet Beach and Chao Loud Beach** is a place of beautiful sunset where you can go for swimming.
- ❏ Visit the fisherman villages and their livings along the Pak Nam Khaem Nu Chalerm Phra Kiat Bridge.
- ❏ Discover the sea breaks; the length is 700 meters, at Bang Chan of Kloong District.
- • Splash in a basin of cool and clear water at Phlio Waterfall in Namtok Phlio National Park; it's a mountainous rainforested National Park which full of streams, waterfalls and rich wildlife. You must trail at the nature trail and relax at a coffee shop there.
- ❏ Adventure Khao **Khitchakut National Park** and hike along Krathing Waterfall; 13 -tier waterfall. This mountain is famous for Buddha's Footprint Pillar; where the Buddhist worshippers believe that if you arrive at this point, you will get luck and happiness. The place is very crowded both day and night during the worshipping festival in Jan-Mar every year.
- ❏ Reach the horizon of Thailand at Pha Hin Koop or the Hin Koop Cliff at Soy Dao Mountainous areas; the wildlife sanctuary. "Koop" means elephant's back. You have to trail for 6-7 kilometers in the forest. Please contact the National Park Office for advanced booking.

- ❏ Namtok Khao Soy Dao is a 16-tier waterfall where you can hike for 2 hours along the layers of this beautiful waterfall. Right now, the park allows tourists to hike only to 9th tier which is about 3 kilometers from the ground.
- ❏ Discover the stunning and beautiful Grand Canyon of Chanthaburi at Nong Bua.
- ❏ Swim with dolphins at the Oasis Sea World. It's the marine park where the dolphins perform in the show and the park also allows guests to play with them closely.
- ❏ Ride the boat to **Ko Proet**; a small island near the shore situated in Laem Sing District area. Homestays are available.
- ❏ Boating and see the flock of red hawk at Bang Chan Low Key Riverfront. The best time is 3 Pm to see many hawks around and see also the local living of fisherman villagers which still keep their unique way of life in the natural surroundings.
- ❏ **The Chanthabul Riverfront Community is the** nice and beautiful ancient markets and houses. The place received The Asia-Pacific-Heritage Award from UNESCO.

Figure 205 Chanthabul riverfront community

- **The Cathedral of Immaculate Conception Chanthaburi**
  Admire **the Cathedral of Immaculate Conception Chanthaburi**; the prominent gothic-style Catholic Church founded in 1909.
- Shop jewelry at Gems Market of Chanthaburi; the biggest gem market in Thailand, Ruby of Siam was found in Chanthaburi and become well known in the world. The market is located at Trirat Road in town.
- Wat Khao Sukim; a famous temple among Thai Buddhists is on the hill in Tha Mai District. You should visit this temple.

❑ See **Khuk Khi Kai**; the former small square prison in 1893 which was built by France. Chanthaburi was occupied by France on the dispute of the land in the left side of Maekong River. The prison was for torturing prisoners by keeping the chickens in a coop on the top of the brick tower with 2 ventilations so the excrement of chicken fell down all the time to prisoners. This ancient prison is situated at Laem Sing District.

Let's go to Trat for admiring many beautiful islands.

Figure 206 Ko Chang

TRAT

Figure 207 Ko Chang Town

❑ Trat is a small coastal province in the east of Thailand. This little town borders Chanthaburi and Cambodia, and The Gulf of Thailand at the south. In fact, it's the tourist destination for many islands like, **Ko Chang, Ko Kut, Ko Kham, Ko Mak, Ko Rang, Ko wai** and so on.

There are flights to Trat everyday or you can catch the bus at The Aekamai Bus Terminal, or from the Suwannaphum Airport on the 1st floor gate no.8, or taxi/car.

If you intend to explore the east coastal towns, you should start from Pattaya City, Rayong, Chanthaburi and end with Trat. It's about 315 kilometers from Bangkok or takes 3-4 hours riding there.

❑ Explore Trat Town by visiting Trat National Museum. The building of this Museum is still maintained its original Thai style since 1922. It's a good place for learning the traditional Thai livings, cultures and historical background of Trat Province.

❑ See the Chinese architecture of the City Pillar Shrine; the center of Trat's people, for both Thai and Chinese worshippers.

❑ Visit the old temple; **Wat Buppharam**, built during Ayutthaya Period for admiring the arts of mural paintings, the sculpture of Buddha Image and many ancient artifacts were found here.

❑ Walk around the community of Bang Phra Canal or **"Klong Bang Phra";** where there are many old wooden houses and commercial buildings.

❑ Discover a wonderful huge mangrove forests of more than 100 years old situated nearby town. It's the Eco System Learning Center Ban Tha Ra Neh. You should ride a small boat to admire these forests.

❑ **Check in a resort at Ko Chang** and take a one day trip for enjoying snorkeling, the coral reefs and beautiful creatures under the crystal clear sea. You must explore the four islands; Ko Rang Islands, Ko Wai, Ko Yak Yai and Ko Yak Lek. Fun sliding from the ship!

  ❑ Ride a boat along canal to see the fisherman-village at **Ban Nam Chiew**.

❑ Enjoy walking on **the black sand beach** at Had Sai Dum of Laem Ngop District.

❑ Taste the sweet **Salack** Fruits at the garden and try also one of Thai desserts made from this fruit, it's called Sala Loy Keaw; it's the Salack fruit seed-removed, mixed with some syrup and ground ice on top. It's awesome to have in summer.

Figure 208 Ko Chang Beach

❑ # Ko Chang is the largest island in The Gulf of Thailand and the 2nd largest island; next from Phuket. "Chang" means Elephant. The island named from its size because normally Thai compares big things or places to elephant, the huge animal.

Ko Chang is full of resorts and hotels which are more comfortable than other islands but you can also have time to explore many beautiful islands around; Trat is called "The province of Islands"; there are 66 islands here.

Ferry-Piers to Ko Chang are at Ao Thammachart Pier and Center Point Pier at Laem Ngop. It takes about 45 minutes to one hour ride but you can enjoy nice view from the deck.

Pier to Ko Kut is at Laem Sork. The minibus for Trat to Ko Kut is available at Suwannaphum International Airport at the 1st floor, gate no. 8, the fare of the trip include ferry trip to the island. You can enjoy all islands during staying somewhere in Trat or one of the islands.

❑ Snorkel around the coral reefs at **Ko Koot** in cystal clear sea water and beautiful natural creations. There are resorts and hotels in Ko Kut for anyone who prefers peace and less crowded than Ko Chang.

• Discover a beautiful waterfall at Ko Kut; Namtok **Klong Chao**, you can enjoy swimming in a big basin of clear and fresh water from waterfall.

• Walk around the fisherman village in Ko Koot and have a nice seafood here.

❑ Take one day trip for exploring **Ko Rang Islands**; the paradise of snorkeling, one of activities at Ko Kut.

❑ Adventure and enjoy snorkeling at **Ko Wai**. Along the way to Ko Wai, you may drop a while at Ko Laoya; find a hut nearby the sea for attaching the nature and cool breeze. It's a wonderful landscape for trailing.

❑ Experience staying in Fishermen's Homestays at **Ko Mai Si Yai Homestay** in the middle of the sea near Ko Chang. (Ride a fisherman-boat at Sutthi Pier in Trat to Ko Mai Si Yai about an hour) Enjoy many activities of fishermen's living.

Lean back and Chill!

EXPLORE ISLANDS

- Thailand is one of the Southeast Asia countries on the mainland of Indochina Peninsula. The country connects The Gulf of Thailand at the south and The Andaman Sea at the west. The total length of Thai coast is 3,148 kilometers. There are many beautiful beaches and islands for exploring in Thailand.

- The best time to tour at Andaman coast; Phuket, Krabi, Satoon, Ranong, Trang and Phang Nga, is in Jan-Apr or Nov-Dec.

- The good time for the south sea by the Gulf of Thailand coast; Suratthani, Chumpon, Nakonsithammarat, Songkla, Pattani, Narathiwat and Pattalung, is about Apr-Oct.

- The best time for tours at the eastern and western coast of the Gulf of Thailand; Trat, Chonburi, Rayong, Pattaya, Chantaburi, Prachup, Hua Hin, and Cha Am is about in Jan-Apr and Nov-Dec.

1 PHUKET

Phuket is the biggest island in Thailand located in Andaman Sea, travel about 900 kilometers from Bangkok. There are 39 islands of Phuket Province. It was assumed found since 2nd Century from the archaeological evidences such as ancient tools and weapons showing that there's humans lived at least since 3000 years ago. Mr. Claudius Ptolemy; a navigator mentioned in his records about this land; it's the long cape, called Takola Cape, from Phan Gna Province, but due to the movement of the fault of a large crust known as Klong Marui Fault; which stretches from Surathani and Phang Nga down to the east of Phuket. The wind waves eroded the soil land to the sea and cut the Takola Cape from the mainland to become a narrow channel between Phuket and Phang Nga. It's called Pak Phra Straits; where the deepest part of the sea here is 8-9 meters nowadays.

Phuket is called from the foreigners and ancient people in the past; as Takola, Jungceylon, Manikram, Phuket, Thalang and Thung Kha.
Phuket is the center destination of Andaman Sea for tourists from all over the world. There are many hotels, resorts, guest houses, houses for rent with facilities. All water sports are available almost everywhere in Phuket; scuba diving, snorkeling, swimming, fishing, surfing and nature trails. There are about 39 islands belong to the Phuket Island Groups such as; Ko Racha Yai, Ko Hey, Ko Kaew, Ko Bon, Ko Ma Prow, Ko Rang Yai, Ko Rang Noi and Ko Mai Ton; which are also tourist attractions during visiting Phuket Province.

Travel here by plane, rail and road.

Figure 209 Laem Phromthep, Phuket

2 SAMUI

The island was known since Ayutthaya period. It's now a district belongs to Suratthani Province, locates in the Gulf of Thailand by the east, away from Suratthani about 84 kms, but from Donsak Pier about 27 kms. It connects Ko Phagnan at the north, the Gulf of Thailand at the east, the sea at Khanom District at the south and Donsak at the west. Travel by plane, by road and continue with ferry at Donsak Pier, express boat and night boat from Ban Don takes about 7-8 hours.

Figure 210 Samui Island

3 PHA GNAN

It's a district belongs to Suratthani Province, away from Suratthani about 100 kilometer. King Rama V visited the island and gave names for the waterfalls here; Tharnsadet, Tharnprapas and Pravej Waterfalls since 1888. It is a beautiful island at the southwest of Thailand, well known for Full Moon Party at Rin Beach.

Figure 211 Ko Pha Gnan, Suratthani

4 KO TAO

The island was named "Tao"; which means "Turtle", because there were many turtles found in this island.

Ko Tao was abandoned island and it's a prison for political prisoners in the past. It was opened and allowed residents in 1947. The island is unique beautiful beaches and crystal clear sea water. It's known among tourists for scuba diving points; which are Kong Hin Chumpon, Hinbai and Kong Hin Toongku, belongs to Suratthani and is about 45 Kms. from Pha Gnan Island. Travel here can be done by planes, trains, buses, and cars to Suratthani and connect ferry boats here.

5 KO NANG YUAN

Ko Nang Yuan is about 500 meters next to Ko Tao. You can go from Ko Tao by speed boat.There are three small islands connected by sand beaches when the sea opens, it's where you can walk among the islands of Ko Yuan. It's a nice island for snorkeling.

Figure 212 Ko Tao and Nang Yuan

6 ANGTHONG

Angthong Islands are groups of islands of Angthong National Marine Park of Thailand. It belongs to Suratthani; away from Ko Samui and Pha Gnan about 20 Kms. The islands are about 42 islands which are mostly lime stone hills with 10-400 meter high and formed in different shapes to become caves and cliffs. Travel to Angthong Islands by ferry boats at Nathon and Bophut Piers in Ko Samui.

You can stay at Ko Wuo Talab, one of Angthong Islands or connect the National Park Office.

Figure 213 Angthong Islands

7 KO PHALUAI

The island belongs to the Group of Angthong Islands. It's known as "Virgin" island with green energy where you can still touch the nature with clean surroundings and fresh air. Travel here by fisherman boats at Donsak, Suratthani and can stay at homestay here.

Figure 214 Ko Phaluai

8 TAPU OR JAMES BOND ISLAND

"Tapu" means "Metal Spike" was the name called the island; which is a tall islet, locates near Khao Phing Kan; the limestone karst islands of Ao Phang Nga National Park in Phang Gna Province. It's famous from Jame Bond Movie in 1974; "The Man with the Golden Gun" series, and becomes the landmark of Phang Nga province which seems to be well known all over the world. Travel here from the tour boats at Surakul Pier.

9 LANTA ISLANDS NATIONAL PARK

Lanta islands is a big group of islands and become a district of Krabi Province; consist of many islands, but the biggest is Ko Lanta Yai; where many people live, the rest which are attractions; such as, Ko Rok Nai, Ko Rok Nok, Ko Ta La Beng and Ko Gnai. The fishermen villages have been living here and keeping old traditions for more than hundred years. Travel here from Bangkok are by planes, buses, cars and connect boats to the island at Chao Fa and Saladan Piers about 2 hrs. Let's see dolphins swim during cool season; January-February!

10 PHI PHI DON & PHI PHI LEY

Phi Phi Islands are part of Had Nopparath Thara National Park; the distance is about 40 kms from Krabi Province. The island was called by locals "Pulao Phiarphi" which means the kind of sea plants and finally called Phi Phi. The groups of islands are Phi Phi Don, Phi Phi Ley and some small islands. The big ones are Phi Phi Don and Ley. The Phi Phi Don Island is a large center with many hotels, resorts with fully facilities and picturesque white sand beaches. It's great for scuba diving and swimming.

11 KO HONG ISLAND KRABI PROVINCE

Ko Hong or called as Ko Lao Bireh. It locates in Tharn Bok Khoranee National Park; consist of many islands. The beautiful beaches here are curved bay with lime stone hill and a nature trail on the island. Travel here at Thab Kaek Resort.

12 KO HONG PHANG GNA PROVINCE

Ko Hong is a large island and can pass through its caves or tidal lagoon which is about 2-10 meter wide and 150 meter depth. It locates in Ao Phang Gna National Marine Park. Most of tourists explore by kayaking through its caves during an appropriate level of tides. Please always check.

Ko Hong is near Pan Yi, Ta Poo Islands. Travel from Tah Dan Pier in Ta Kua Thung District.

Figure 215 Ko Hong

13 KO KRADAN

Ko Kradan has the most beautiful beach in Trang province. The island is about 10 Kms. from the southeast coast of Thailand. The main parts of island belong to Hat Chao Mai National Marine Park, with 2 Kms. Long beach. The island is very well known to the world-famous underwater weddings, which is held during February every year. It was recorded in the Guinness Book of World Records as the largest underwater wedding in the world. Travel here from Pak Meng Pier about 30 minutes.

Figure 216 Ko Kradan

Figure 217 Ko Pan Yi

14 KO PAN YI

Ko Pan Yi was found about 200 years ago by Indonesian. It's known as the amazing fishermen Village in the sea; about 200 homes, of Phang Nga Province. The island has been very popular and nice to explore. It's mostly for lunch stop for package tours. One of the major attractions is an amazing football field on the sea here. Travel here at Thadan Sullakakon Pier.

15 KO SIMILAN

"Similan" means "Nine", the islands are 9 islands in Similan Islands Group of National Marine Park in Phang Gna.It's about 70 kms.from Thablamu Pier in Phan Gna and 90 kms. from the pier of Patong beach in Phuket. It's called as "Heaven of Andaman Sea" where there are many corals, rare fish. The best time to come here is in Nov-Apr.

Figure 218 Ko Similan

16 KO SURIN ISLANDS

Ko Surin Islands are Surin Islands National Marine Park in Phang Nga Province. It borders Myanmar in Andaman Sea and away from the western coast about 70 Kilometers. Ko Surin Group is 5 islands and has a stunning seaview with coral reefs, forests and white sand beaches. Travel here from Kuraburi Pier about 1.5 hours. You can do "One day trip" or stay overnight at Ao Chong Kard" of Ko Surin Nua.

Figure 219 Ko Surin

17   KO KAI

Ko Kai is one of 4 island trip for tourists; Ko Porda, Ko Thub, Ko Mor and Ko Kai. "Kai" means "Hen"; some said it looks like hen's head. The tourists swim and enjoy at Porda Island where there are resorts and great white sand beach. The four islands are popular in the sea of Krabi.

Figure 220 Ko Kai

18   KO PHAYAM

Ko Phayam is a beautiful island in Ranong Province which is about 600 kms from Bangkok. Travel to Ranong can be done by buses, cars, rails and by planes. You can ride the boat from Paknam Pier to Ko Phayam. It's the island with a wide beach. There are bungalows and resorts around the island.

Figure 221 Ko Phayam

19 KO LI PE

Start your trip at Pakbara Pier in Satoon Province for about 67 kms to Ko Li Pe. The island is near the border to Malaysia. It's a part of Talutao National Marine Park. It's famous for scuba diving and beautiful white sand beach. You can also enjoy Walking Street here. The popular beach is called Pattaya Beach where you can find many hotels, restaurant and Walking Street in the late afternoon. Travel to Ko Li Pe with exploring other interesting small islands along the way like; Ko Khai, Ko Hin Gnam, snorkeling at Jabang Point to see corals, Ko Ravee for enjoying the clear water, Ko Phueng, and also can snorkeling at Ko Hinson.

Figure 222Ko Li Pe

20 KO TALUTAO

Ko Talutao was the prison in 1936 for serious prisoners. It's the biggest island of Talutao National Marine Park; which are 51 islands in Andaman Sea, locates in Satoon Province near Langkawi Island of Malaysia. Travel here from Pakbara Pier in Satoon.

Figure 223 Ko Talutao

21 KO CHANG

The island is at the east of the Gulf of Thailand, located in Trat. It's the 3rd biggest island in Thailand; next from Ko Samui and Ko Phuket. Please see details of Ko Chang in **Trat Page no**.

22 KO KUT

The island is 4th largest in Thailand and located at the end of the eastern sea in Trat. You can travel from Laem Sork Pier in Trat or planes to Soneva Kiri Airport or Ko Mai Si from Suwannaphum Airport. The best time for this island is in Oct-May.

Figure 224 Ko Kut

23 KO MAK

The island locates between Ko Chang and Ko Kut. It's about 39 kilometers from the shore; having the length of beach about 27 kilometers. There are coral reefs found perfectly in the island area. Many hotels, a temple, market and a health center are here. You can also walk to Ko Kham from here.

Figure 225 Ko Mak

24 KO LAN

Ko Lan is a popular island for those who visit **Pattaya City in Chonburi** Province. It's only 7.5 kms from Pattaya beach, located in the Gulf of Thailand, having Ko Sak and Ko Krok is in group of islands. Ko Lan was originally a subdistrict and inhabitaed for a long time by farming and fishing before; but because of being robbed by the pirates and Cholera disease during the World War II and in addition to inconvenient transportation here; therefore, Ko Lan was dissolved and merged to Nakrua Subdistrict and become part of Pattaya City in 1978.

You can come here by speed boat or ferry boat at Laem Balihay Pier (7 am-18.00pm). If you prefer to stay here, the accommodations are available. People enjoy Ko Lan at Ta Waen Beach, Sang wan Beach, Thong Lang Beach, Ta Yai Beach, Samae Beach, Tien Beach, Nuan Beach, Khao Nom View Point and Kang Han Lom View Point.

Figure 226 Ko Lan

25 KO KHAM

This is an island of crystal clear water and a white sand beach which is well known for Underwater Park; a beautiful sea of Sattaheep in Chonburi Province. It's popular beach and sea near Bangkok. (2 hours by car)

Figure 227 Ko Kham

26 KO SAMAE SAN

The island is for one day trip in Sattaheep. There are activities, such as, snorkeling, kayaking, biking and walking along nature trail. The last boat for return to the land is at 16.00 PM.

Figure 228 Ko Samae San

27 KO SAMET

The island is upper part of the gulf of Thailand, locates at Ban Phe in Rayong Province. The area of island is full of jungle and mountains. There are many beautiful bays and beaches with hotels and resorts in the island.

Figure 229 Ko Samet

28 KO THALU

Ko Thalu is the first sea for snorkeling before going to the south. It's a wonderful island of the Gulf of Thailand, locates in Prachub Khiri Khun Province which is about 400 kms. from Bangkok Travel here from Had Laem Son Pier for 30 minutes by speed boat.

Figure 230 Ko Thalu

29 KO LANKA JEW

Ko Lanka Jew is a bird's nest concession island, part of Mu Ko Chumporn National Marine Park in Chumporn Province. The coastal coral reefs appearing on the western side of the island are still in very good condition. It's a restricted area but you can visit for day trip 8.00-17.00.

Figure 231 Ko Lanka Jew

CHIANG MAI

❑ Visit Chiang Mai in winter time here is terrific; it's in between November-February, the weather is fine and cold. Chiang Mai is the 2nd biggest province; next to Bangkok, in Thailand. The province is full of many attractions; for both nature and the city-life, where you can enjoy all year round. It is surrounded by the mountain ranges of the Thai highlands; with Doi Inthanon; the highest mountain with 2,565 meter high, dense forests and many national parks are popular tourist attractions. The distance from Bangkok to Chiang Mai is about 700 kilometers.

HOW DO YOU GO TO CHIANG MAI?

- **By Plane**; Chiang Mai International Airport is the major gateway to the northern region of Thailand. You can fly directly or by domestic flights at Suwannaphum and Don Muang Airports.
- **By car**; you can follow the route along Asia Road from Rangsit passing Ayutthaya and heading direct to Nakhon Sawan, Kham Phaeng Phet, Tak, Lampang, Lamphun and Chiang Mai. It takes about 7 hours to reach downtown.
- **By bus**; at the Northern Bus Terminal at Mo Chit, Bangkok. Or from the bus terminal in each province.
- **By train**; at Hua Lumphong Railway Station along the Northern Line. You have to book advance ticket for a sleeper train and enjoy in a Thai train.
- **By package tour**s; at the tour service counters at the airport so you can understand what you want to go and see.
- By public transportations from province to province; wherever you want to stop and stay overnight; looking around Thailand up to the north may take about 2-3 weeks, there are buses in every province to go.
- **Book a Green Bus for Chiang Mai - Chiang Rai-Chiang Mai.**

    Chiang Mai is a province of a long history. It was a capital of The Lanna Kingdom.
"Lan Na" means "The Land of Million Fields" or from some evidences means "The Land of Rice Fields", depends on the calling; if pronounced in higher tone "Lant" means "Million"; but if in lower tone, "Lan" means "Courtyard".

Lan Na Kingdom was an ancient kingdom from 13th -18th Centuries. In the past; the kingdom belonged to Yuan; or called as "Tai Yuan"; a Thai ethnic group which native to the 8 provinces of the northern region; Lamphun, Lampang, Phrae, Nan, Phayao, Mae Hong Sorn, Chiang Rai and Chiang Mai, included Xishuangbanna Dai Autonomous Prefecture; Jinghong in the south of Yunnan. They had their own language, alphabets, culture and tradition. The parts of Lan Na Kingdom now are in Thailand, Myanmar, Laos and China.

**When you are in Chiang Mai, you should start to learn how to know the city by riding local transports like Rode Song Thaew and stop wherever you like, hire a motorcycle or by walking.

❑ **Ride Rode Song Taew**; a standard pick-up truck modified its rear for 2 row-seats with higher roof and registered as a local transport for passengers in downtown. "Song Taew" means "2 rows" and "Rode" means "any kind of cars can be called

"Rode" in Thai. Rode Song Taew is normally found in every province and some areas in Bangkok. They are found all over in Chiang Mai and convenient for you to roam around the town or some nearby districts.

Figure 232 Rode Song Thaew

Figure 233 Doi Suthep, Chiang Mai

❑ **Explore Doi Suthep - Doi Pui National Park**; a beautiful mountainous landscape which is a part of **Thanon Thong Chai Range**; the range has many hills; such as, Doi Suthep, Doi Buak Ha and Doi Pui. The highest peak is Doi Pui; 1,676 meter high. **Activities** in the park is hiking, cycling, camping and walking around for exploring many historical attractions located in the areas.

What will you explore?

Figure 234 Khru Ba Si Wichai statue at Lamphun province

❑ Admire **Khru Ba Si Wichai Memorial** at the entrance
to Wat Doi Suthep. Khru Ba Si Wichai was a highly
respected northern Thai Buddhist monk who best
known for building many constructions of Buddhist
temples included **Wat Phra Thart Doi Suthep;** he led
the northern people in constructing the road to the
sacred pagoda successfully.

❑ Admire a beautiful golden pagoda **at Wat Phra Thart
Doi Suthep**; situated 15 kilometers from downtown and
about 689 meters high from the plain land, about an
elevation of 1,046 meters. It's a national archaeological
site and one of the destinations for Thai Buddhists
because the pagoda contains Buddha's Relic; a sacred
place for worshipping Buddha and become a landmark
of Chiang Mai.

The original pagoda was built for Buddha's Relic
in 1369 but it was restored and re-constructed many times
until Khru Ba Si Wichai came and restored the pagoda and
the ordination hall in 1920 and built the road to Doi Suthep
in 1934. The road to the pagoda is named after his name;
called Si Wichai Road.

Walk around and see many beautiful items such as; the Buddha statues, the Bell Tower, Bells and Hindu God in the temple areas. You can see a nice view of Chiang Mai Town from the temple. **Please dress modestly.**

❑ Admire the Thai architectural "Group of Houses" Central Style of Art at **Bhubing Palace**; the royal residence on the hill at Doi Buak Ha which is about 1,373 meter high above sea level and its location is a part of Chiang Mai Town.

The palace was built in 1961 in the reign of King Bhumibol; who also gave the palace's name. It's for the royal residence during visiting Chiang Mai and the nearby provinces and also used as a guesthouse for their foreign visitors.

This palace is about 4 kilometers from Doi Suthep and about 17 kilometers from town.

❑ **Visit Doi Suthep Nature Center**; a place for learning about Doi Suthep; for its nature and historical places, you can get information for traveling around.

❑ **See Huay Kaew Waterfall** near the entrance to Doi Suthep.

❑ **See Montha Tharn Waterfall**; a beautiful 3-tier waterfall above Huay Kaew Waterfall.

❑ **See Mae Sa Waterfall; a** beautiful and famous 10-tier waterfall of Chiang Mai, it's convenient to reach this waterfall.

❑ **See many Cliffs**; Pha Gnerb, Pha Lad, Pha Wang Bua Ban, Pha Dam where you can see a beautiful views of Chiang Mai.

❑ **Hike to Doi Pui**; the height is 1,676 meters where the weather is cold and windy but you can see the picturesque landscape surroundings.

❑ **Visit the hill tribe villages**; where you can enter to many groups of them.

❑ **See Phra thart Doi Kham at Wat Phrathart Doi Kham;** located on the hill where the pagoda enshrined Buddha's Relic on the top. This temple is about 1300 years old; one the oldest temples in Chiang Mai. It's not so far from downtown.

Figure 235 Wat Phra Sing, Chiang Mai

❑ Visit **Wat Phra Singh**; "Singh" means "Lion", at the entrance, there are lion statues as guards. The temple was built about in 1345 and situated inside the city wall and it's the temple where **Phra Phutta Sihing is situated as** the principal Buddha and one of the main centers for Chiang Mai Buddhist people come for worshipping.
There are many beautiful viharn halls and mural paintings inside the temple.

Figure 236 Wat Chedi Luang, Chiang Mai

- ❏ Admire a beautiful large Pagoda at **Wat Chedi Luang**; an old temple built in 14th Century and announced as The National Historic Site in 1925. It's located at the center of Chiang Mai. The square pagoda base is 60 meter wide but the pagoda peak was ruined by lightning left only seen at the present.
- ❏ Visit **Chiang Mai National Museum**.
- ❏ Enjoy the W**alking Street** on Saturday along Wua Lai Road.
- ❏ Enjoy the areas of Tha Pae Gate to Wat Phra Singh Walking Street on Sunday.
- ❏ See the location of Chiang Mai University at **Nim Marn Haemin Road**; the well known areas for many entertainments and hotels among tourists.

Figure 237 Umbrellas by local handmade

❑ Visit **San Kamphaeng District** areas; the east of Chiang Mai and connected to Lamphune Province at the south. It's about 15 kilometers from Chiang Mai downtown.

❑ Spa at the hot springs in **San Kamphaeng Hot Springs**; a place for picnic and relaxation.

❑ Shop at **Bo Sang Umbrella Village**; the center for umbrella making and handicrafts center.

❑ Walk down a staircase to a large cave hall with beautiful stalagmites and stalactites at **Tham Muang On** in Mae On District. This cave is at a limestone mountain surrounded by a mountain range. There's a sacred Buddha's relic or called as Phra Thart Nompha situated at the center of the cave.

Figure 238 Mae Kam Phong Village, Chiang Mai

❏ Explore **Mae Kampong Village** in Mae On District which is about 50 kilometers from Chiang Mai Town. This village is famous among tourists as a little town with many homestays. The roads to the village are quiet steep and narrow with many curves. If you don't want to drive, you can ride a local bus for coming here. There are natural beautiful scenery and old temples.

❏ **Stay overnight at a homestay** in Mae Kampong Village.

❏ **Trail walk** along the areas in Mae Kampong Village and **Hike** along the nature trails to **Mae Kampong Waterfall**.

- ❏ **Eat grilled "Sai Oua",** the famous local northern sausages; the ground meat is mixed with chilli paste and herbal plants and spice added.
- ❏ Admire a teak wood carving at the hall of **Wat Kantha Pruksa** or called by local is **Wat Mae Kampong** which built in 1930. It's the center and sacred site for the villagers' worshipping.
- ❏ Discover a beautiful Lanna architecture from a little hall in the middle of stream.

Figure 239Mae Kampong, Chiang Mai

- ❏ Visit **Chiang Mai Zoo and Aquarium**; located near Doi Suthep, not only variety of animals but there is an archaeological site found within the area of the zoo; it's called Wat Khu Din Khao, the site was an old Lanna ancient town.
- ❏ See the architectural design at the entrance of the Zoo in three languages; Lanna, English and Thai.
- ❏ Discover a **beautiful Pavilion** at the **Royal Park Rajapruek;** which is the royal pavilion built during the grand celebrations hosted by the Royal Thai Government in honor of King Bhumibol who is the world's longest reigning monarch. It was a place for horticultural exposition during 2006-2007.

Figure 240 The Royal Park Rajapruek, Chiang Mai

❑ Discover **Chiang Mai Night Safari near The Royal Park Rajapruek**; believed that it's the first nocturnal zoo in Thailand and the largest in the world. Many activities from the zoo such as; Digital zoo with technology for games, the buses drive around during the night, ride a tram during the daytime, taking care animals and walking track around the lake for seeing animals and the musical fountain show. Resort is available here.

Figure 241 The Three Kings Monument, Chiang Mai

❑ See **the Three Kings Monument**; King Mang Rai, Phaya Gnam Muang and Por Khun Ram Kham Haeng Maharaj, who established Chiang Mai City. The monument is at the center of town.

❑ The Night Bazarr is full of shops, restaurants, café and entertainment. It's nice to walk around the areas at night but you have to be careful for your bags and pockets.

- ❏ Enjoy night life in Chiang Mai.

- ❏ See **Mae Ping River;** the main river originated in Chiang Dao District and flow passing in Chiang Mai Town to other provinces and forms The Chao Phraya River, the main river of Thailand.

Figure 242 Tha Pae Gate

- ❏ **See the Tha Pae Gate**; it was original called "Chiang Rueak Gate" which was believed it's the inside city wall for protecting the city in the past. This gate plan was rebuilt in 1985 from old historical evidences of Tha Pae Gate which was the outside wall which become ruined.

  The local people call the rebuilt of the inside city wall as **Tha Pae Gate** since then.

- ❏ Walk around in **Waroroth Market**; a local market which is famous for local food and fabrics. In local northern language; "Khard" means "Market", so you may hear the local say **"Khard Waroroth"** instead.

❑ Visit **Baan Tawai Handicraft Village**; a center of handmade wooden products which is famous for local craftsmanship. The items sold here are from small pieces as a souvenir to large furniture that you order and take home. Ban Tawai locates in **Hang Dong District.** **When you reach Chiang Mai, you must go to Doi Inthanon and explore these mountainous areas at least once.**

Figure 243 The road up to Doi Inthanon

> ➤ Reach the top of **Doi Inthanon** in **Chom Thong District**; the highest mountain in Thailand. The old name was called "Doi Luang" but changed to honor a king of Chiang Mai whose name was Phra Chao In-tha-wit-cha-ya-non, who tried to preserve the forests within the city.

ADVENTURE IN DOI INTHANON:

The height of Doi Inthanon is 2,565 meters above sea level. There are two beautiful pagodas on this hill for honoring King Bhumibol built in 1987 and Queen Sirikit in 1992 near the summit of Doi Inthanon. The hill is popular for tourists during cool season; November-February, the temperature may sometimes drop to $0°$

> ➤ Admire the beautiful green fields of rice terraces in **Baan Mae Klang Luang** at the 26th kilometer point or 5 kilometers from Doi Inthanon National Park Office.

❑ Trail along the rainforests for breathtaking mountain views at **Kew Mae Pan Nature Trail**; a heaven on earth in the area of Doi Inthanon National Park.

❑ Enjoy hiking at a **spectacular Pha Dok Sieo Nature Trail** and discover a beautiful waterfall and stream in Doi Inthanon National Park.

❑ Trail in **Ang Ka Nature Trail**; walk along a board walk through the rainforest of Doi Inthanon.

❑ Admire picturesque botanical garden of winter plants, fruits, flowers and vegetables nearby the hillsides and enjoy walking around at **The Royal Agricultural Station Inthanon, Gate house.**

❑ Relax at Homestay in **Baan Mae Klang Luang.**

❑ **Sleep in a tent** in Doi Inthanon National Park.

❑ **Enjoy a delicious Thai meal and a fresh salad** from the royal garden Station at Inthanon Royal Project Restaurant

Discover one of the best viewpoint **at Doi Mon Mark.**; the scenic hill for beautiful sunrise and sunset. It's about between Mae Chaem District and Doi Inthanon.

❑ See a beautiful **Pine Park at Wat Chan Royal Project**; located at **Kalayaniwattana District**, a development center initiated by His Majesty King Bhumibol, during his visiting the villagers, for cultivation and improve the infrastructure in the Baan Wat Chan Community.

❑ See **Wat Huai Hom**; a small temple in Baan Chan of Kalayaniwattana District.

❑ Discover a beautiful Grand Canyon of Thailand at **Pha Chor** in Mae Wang National Park; a forest park covers Doi Lor, Chom Thong and Mae Wang Districts with highlands about 400-1900 meter high, home of many wildlife.

❏ Hike and walk along **Pha Chor nature trails** to see Pha Chor; the amazing natural phenomena of rock formation, recommended in cool season for visiting; between Nov-Jan. "Pha" means " Slope"

Figure 244 Pha Chor, Chiang Mai

❏ Discover 50,000 dolls collected at **Chiang Mai Doll Museum and Factory** in **San Patong District**, 20 kilometers to the south of Chiang Mai Town. The museum has varieties of Thai dolls and thousands of dolls from all over the world. It's the center for handmade doll-making. Visit **Wiang Tha Kan**; an archaeological site in San Patong District built about in 16th Century consists of city walls, pagodas and ruined temples.

❑ Bath elephants and walk into the jungle with them at **Elephant Freedom Project** in Mae Wang District area. Mae Wang areas cover many national parks and many tourist attractions such as; rafting, camping and nature trails in the park.

❑ Discover a beautiful complete Lanna architectural Hall; amazing wood carving at Wat **Ton Kwane or Wat Inthrawath**; an ancient Lanna temple built about in 1846, located in Hang Dong District.

MAE CHAEM

- ❏ Visit **Mae Chaem** District during Nov-Feb for a cool weather; located at the west of Chiang Mai where there are many ancient temples, waterfalls, hot spring and beautiful forest.
- ❏ **Admire "Koo Prasat"**; a beautiful plaster carving decorated behind the Buddha image in the main hall of Wat Yang Luang; a temple near Wat Pa Daed in the center of **Mae Chaem District.**

There's a famous old tradition; called "Jul Khatin" in this temple. This is an old tradition after Buddhist Lent day. It's a process for making monk-robe; started from the preparation of cotton, for offering to the monk and it's all done by the people in community or village.It aims for harmony and merits together.

❑ Experience with elephants in natural behaviors in a beautiful areas of **BEES Elephant Sanctuary at Ban Thung Yaw** in Mae Chaem District. You can join the program for observing, caring, making food for elephants and participate in helping other rescued animals.

❑ To be impressed with the unique Lanna architectural style at **Wat Pa Daed Complex in Mae Chaem. T**he temple is famous for beautiful mural paintings inside the Viharn Hall depicted the Buddha's life. It's built about 1857 but still looked completely.

❑ Shop a unique northern style fabric at **The Traditional Cotton Woven Village** in Tha Pha, Mae Chaem District.

❑ Visit Mae Rim District; a large district with many government offices and tourist attractions. A part of Doi Suthep is in Mae Rim District. Ride Song Thaew to Mae Rim for many places of nature and culture.

❑ Enjoy walking around **The Queen Sirikit Botanical Garden**; Thailand's largest glasshouse complex with 12 greenhouses.

❑ Visit **Princess Sirindhorn Astro Park**; a center for technology and innovation of astrology located in Mae Rim, include planetarium, observatory and exhibitions of astrology for learning and experiencing.

❑ Admire **Darapirom Palace Museum Chulalongkorn**; a beautiful wooden building palace belonged to the Princess; Chao Dara Rathsami, which built in about 1927 located in Mae Rim.

❑ Visit **Wat Pa Darapirom located** nearby Darapirom Palace. The old temple consists of Lanna architectures and sculptures such as; Buddha Statues, Viharn halls, pavilions, mondop, pagoda and stupas with beautiful decorations.

❑ Visit **Wat Phraphutthabat Si Roi**; the four Buddha's footprints are housed in a beautiful pavilion for worshipping. The road to the temple is quiet difficult for driving because it's a long narrow steep road to a high hill where the temple is situated. Although it's not easy to go, but you would see villages, rice fields and natural upcountry landscape of Chiang Mai along the way.

❑ Jog at **the 700th Anniversary Stadium**; a multi purpose stadium of Chiang Mai Province located in Mae Rim.

❑ Discover **Roi-tawarabarn Baan-dha-walai**; a private gallery of amazing arts and Hindu God named Phra Pickhaneth in a shrine. The sculpture of Hindu God is carved in one piece of wood. It's a very interesting small gallery-museum where you can admire many pieces of beautiful artworks; especially, the elegant carving and painting of 100 doors; the meaning of the gallery's name.

❑ Admire Lord Buddha Lanna Square; or called as **Khuang Phra Chao Lanna** or the Buddhist Holy Place, newly built for worshipping and meditating. The place is situated near the entrance to Huay Tueng Thao Reservoir.

❑ Enjoy cycling at **Huay Tueng Thao Reservoir**; the water reservoir look like a lake, a place for chilling and relaxing, eat a local food, swim and enjoy many water sport activities.

❑ Visit a **Snake Farm** in Mae Rim District and see exciting shows.

- ❑ **Photo with lovely tigers** at Tiger Kingdom in Mae Rim, where you see several kinds of tigers.
- ❑ Get excited in extreme activities in **Pongyang Jungle Coaster Zip line Camp and Resort**; a package adventure for zip line, jungle coaster from a hill, quick jump and an exciting cafe.
- ❑ Visit **Mon Jam**; a scenic mountain top farming areas and cool place.
- ❑ Visit **The Orchid Farm in Mae Rim**; seeing many rare orchids, butterflies and Thai cats.
- ❑ Discover **the Long-Neck Karen Hill Tribe Village**; located near Mon Jam, for seeing traditional life of Karen and their clothes with necklaces made their neck  long. Karen Hill Tribe or Kayan people are subgroup of Red Karen in Myanmar, women are well known for wearing neck rings; this is a cultural identity for Karen women. They start wearing rings since 5 years old. Many of Karen people live in Mae Hong Sorn province and the mountainous areas in the north.
- ❑ Visit Mae Sa Elephant Camp; the old elephant camp in Chiang Mai, where you can see the shows, elephants' daily life with their herders and get close to elephants.
- ❑ Have a look at hundreds of insect species at **Siam Insect Zoo** in Mae Rim.
- ❑ **Experience taking care of elephants** and their needs without riding at Maerim Elephant Sanctuary. This is where elephants are happy and respected, founded in 2016 as an elephant conservation project.
- ❑ Splash in **Namtok Mae Sa**; a beautiful 10- tier waterfall with a large basin for swimming. Enjoy nature trails here.

❑ From the snake farm of Mae Rim about 10 kms., you
should hike and refresh at **Namtok Tad Mork**; a
nice waterfall where you can enjoy splashing at the
waterfall and admire a beautiful natural scenery of
forest surroundings.

You can ride along the Chiang Mai-Fang
Route No. 107 from Maerim to Mae Tang District. It's
the road to Pai in Mae Hong Sorn. Let's go to Mae
Tang District.

Figure 245 Wat Aranwiwek, Mae Tang

☐ Visit **Wat Aranyawiwek** on the way to Mae Gnad Dam; the temple has been famous since Phra Ajarn Plien Panyapateepo was alive; he's a forest-monk who lived here for life and widely known among Buddhists in Thailand and foreigners. I came here whenever I visited the north.

☐ Have a boat ride **in Mae Gnad Dam** at **Sri Lanna National Park**; a park with a huge lake where you can stay in a boat house and kayak. The location is in **Mae Tang District** which is next from Mae Rim about 30 kilometers.

- Experience overnight stay in a huge land of elephants at Elephant Nature Park; the most popular and ethical elephant sanctuary owned by Lek Chailert; a lady who is widely known for her conservation work with elephants since 1990. The place has several programs for closing to elephants in the park. This is where the elephants live freely but you can feed them. The huge park is in Mae Tang District and away from town about 65 kilometers.
- Jungle walk along the hill with elephants at **The Karen Elephant Retreat** in Mae Tang District area; one of the projects from The Elephant Nature Park.
- Feed the rescued elephants at **The Happy Elephant Home** at Kuet Chang in Mae Tang District area.

- ❑ Walk around at **Mae Malai Market; a center known for resting before going** further sight-seeing, its location is at the square of Mae Tang District where you can travel to Huai Nam Dang, Pai, Chiang Dao and Fang District; the road heads for Chiang Rai Province.
- ❑ **Explore Huai Nam Dang** National Park; a park of Chiang Mai and Mae Hong Sorn Provinces, the picturesque mountainous areas, a popular rest area for travellers before going to Pai District. Drive carefully along curve steep roads. You can stay here and adventure for caves, waterfalls, hot springs and hills.
- ❑ Discover a very beautiful sea fog and sunrise at **Doi Kio Lom** at Huai Nam Dang.
- ❑ **Mineral Bath at Pong Dueat Geyser;** hot springs in Huai Nam Dang.
- ❑ Visit a very beautiful temple called **Wat Ban Dhen;** on the way to **Mae Gnad Dam;** where you raft and view the beautiful scenery.
- ❑ Trail to **Mork Fa Waterfall** at Sop Poeng, Mae Tang District. This is along the way to Pai District. You can swim in a crystal clear water and hike to the nature.
- ❑ **White water rapids rafting in** inflatable boat along **Mae Tang River;** from Baan Sop Khai to Mae Guet about 3 hours of 10 kilometers for enjoying 14 khaengs or rapids; in September is for professional rafters but during Jan-Mar is a good time for safe rafting with family.
- ❑ **Explore** Chiang Dao District; a nice place next from Mae Tang District. You can catch a local bus from downtown in Chiang Mai here and rent a motor bike for exploring.
- ❑ Ride a motor bike from Chiang Dao Town to **Mae Mae and Muang Khong**.
- ❑ Discover a nice local **homestay at Muang Khong;** a small village hidden in a valley with a beautiful environment located in Chiang Dao District area.

Figure 246 Wat Ban Dhen, Mae Tang

Figure 247 Rural area and Muang Khong

Figure 248 Doi Luang Chiang Dao

- ❏ Hike to **Doi Chiang Dao**; the 3rd highest mountain peak of Thailand, 2,275 meter high above sea level.
- ❏ Explore **Chiang Dao Cave;** a large cave of Chiang Mai with amazing stalactites and a beautiful temple.

❑ Climb the steps up to the large cave on a hill at **Wat Tham Pha Plong in Chiang Dao.** It's a temple where Luang Pu Sim; a well respected monk for introspection among Thai Buddhists, was an abbot of the temple. Feel good with Buddhist quotes along the way up the hilltop. When you reach the cave, you can see a stunning view of forest landscape. Please dress modestly.

❑ Hike to **Namtok Si Sangwan;** a limestone waterfall in Pha Daeng National Park in Chiang Dao District.

❑ Admire **The Stupa of King Naresuan The Great;** this is a monument located in Chiang Dao District, along the way to Doi Ang Khang

❑ Explore **Doi Ang Khang;** a famous mountain located in **Fang District** where the royal agricultural site is situated as a research station; it was set up by King Bhumibol since 1969. The peak Doi Ang Khang is 1,928 meters above sea level. The lowest temperature is -3 Celsius in January. Please drive carefully along many sharp curves. You must visit and stay in a tent on this mountain.

Figure 249 Doi Ang Khang

See a beautiful cherry-blossom flower at Doi Ang Khang.

❑ Discover a beautiful viewpoint of sunrise at **Rai Cha 2000**; this land is a beautiful tea plantation and a fabulous landscape, and also for sipping good quality of tea in a scenic mountain views.

- ❏ Discover an old pagoda of Buddha's Relic at **Phra Thart Doi Ang Khang** by walking along high steps.
- ❏ Discover a meditation house look like a temple in Doi Ang Khang areas.
- ❏ Explore by walking inside **Royal Agricultural Station Ang Khang**; the place you enjoy seeing and picturing many flowers, trees, and vegetables include sakura flowers.
- ❏ See the nice viewpoint at **Doi Ang Khang Military Base.**
- ❏ Check in a tent at **Mon Son Camp Ground and a beautiful Viewpoint** of Doi Ang Khang.
- ❏ Discover Yunnan restaurant with delicious Chinese Style food are served.
- ❏ **See a beautiful strawberry field along the mountain slope at Ban Nor Lae;** Hill Tribe Village located along the border skirt of Thailand and Myanmar.
- ❏ Reach the Peak of Ang Khang Mountain of 1,928 meter high.
- ❏ Discover the beautiful Japanese Kingdom or **Hinoki Land** located in Chai Prakan District areas. The construction of buildings were the replica of the famous original places in Japan which made from Hinoki Trees, you can enjoy wearing Japanese clothes for pictures as if you are in Japan with a stunning view here.

Figure 250 The pathway inside Hinoki Land, Chiang Mai

Figure 251 Wat Tham Tabtao

- ❑ Discover beautiful limestone caves at **Wat Tham Tab Tao; an old temple** in Chai Prakan District area; there are two caves in this temple; called as the dark and the bright caves surrounded by beautiful forests. The caves are large and it takes about an hour for looking around the amazing nature created inside with the sculptures of Buddha statues

- ❑ **Explore Doi Saket**; a district at the east of Chiang Mai and the route to go to Chiang Rai.It'a one of the important districts for business and residential areas. If you ride a motorbike, take the way to Mae Rim and choose to San Sai District, but if coming from the highway; there's a sign for Doi Saket District.

- ❑ Admire a beautiful pagoda on the hill **at Wat Phra Thart Doi Saket**; by climbing steps to reach the top to see a beautiful view of town.

- ❑ **Spa** in a natural hot spring at Ban Pong Samakkee in Doi Saket District.

- ❑ Adventure at **Doi Pha Hom Pok National Park** in Fang District areas, the highest peak is 2,285 meter high. It's the 2nd highest peak next from Doi Inthanon. The park is about 160 kilometers from Chiang Mai downtown.
- ❑ Watch birds at **Doi Lang** in Doi Pha Hom Pok National Park.
- ❑ Discover a geysers rising up to 50 meter high at **Fang Hot Spring** in Doi Pha Hom Pok National Park.
- ❑ **Bath mineral hot spring at Fang Hot Spring**. Admire the beautiful gilded black lacquer on the wall of the ordination hall at **Wat Chedi Gnam**; an old temple in Fang District.
- ❑ Discover **Wat Tha Ton**; an old temple on a hill at Tha Ton a sub-district of **Mae Ai District**; the end route of Chiang Mai and the way to Chiang Rai or Phayao. The beautiful viewpoint of Mae Ai District and mountains are here.

Figure 252 Wat Thaton

Figure 253 Mae Hong Sorn

You can travel to Mae Hong Sorn by airplanes from Chiang Mai for adventure and admire this hidden town in the valley for few days. It's a popular destination from Chiang Mai to explore and relax.

Figure 254 Chiangrai; Wat Rong Khun, Sea fog, the Golden triangle

CHIANGRAI

When you visit Chiang Mai, add Chiangrai in your program because the distance is only about 185 kms or 2 hours ride. It's the northernmost province of Thailand and borders Chiang Mai at the west. Most of the areas are highland and forests. The weather is fine with average about 24 Celsius and some of the areas are cold weather. There are about 27 forest parks for adventure, arboretum, and national reserved forests. Phra Chao Mengrai (1239-1311) established Chiangrai in 1262. He was the first king of Lanna Kingdom who also established Chiang Mai. Many places in the north were named after his name.

The majority of the population is ethnic Thai who speak "Kham Muang Language", hill tribes and Chinese.

Figure 255 Phra Chao Meng Rai Memorial

Figure 256 Mae Khong River in Chiangrai

Chiang Rai borders Myanmar, Laos, Phayao and Chiang Mai. The Fourth Thai-Laos Friendship Bridge over Mekhong River in Chiang Rai is linked to Houayxay in Laos.

How to go to Chiangrai from Bangkok:

❑ Catch a plane to **Chiang Rai**; the northernmost province of Thailand. It's about 1,100 kilometers from Bangkok to this highland province. Going by plane can be the fastest way here.

❑ Ride a bus at the Northern Bus Terminal at Mo Chit to Chiang Rai.

❑ Ride a train from Hua Lumphong Railway Station or Bangsue Grand Station to Chiang Rai.

❏ I always enjoy driving from Bangkok to Chiang Rai. It takes about 8-9 hours. I love to travel by car because there are many places to visit along the way. Sometimes it took for a couple of days to reach Chiangrai by driving, but it's really a fun trip for the northern route and it's worth driving around for exploring the nature, temples and eat local food. You can hire a car from the airport.

❏ You should find a hotel in Chiangrai downtown and walk around before moving to other areas. I think staying in downtown is much easier to find out what you should see and visit. But if you get used to the province well, then you can go to stay close to nature surroundings like hills and hill tribe villages or stay close to the border at Mae sai, Chiang Khong and Chiangsaen for enjoying the differences of beautiful landscape of Chiangrai.

Figure 257 Wat Rong Sue Ten, The Blue Temple

- ❑ Visit **Wat Rong Suea Ten**; or called as **"The Blue Temple"** located on a bank of Kok River in Chiang Rai Town, the home of many beautiful Buddhist Arts in both architectures and sculptures.

- ❑ Visit **Wat Phra Kaew**; the famous temple, the original place of The Emerald Buddha in The Grand Palace in Bangkok. It's in Chiang Rai Town. There are many places inside the temple; such as, the Ordination Hall built in 1890, Phra Chao Lan Thong; the principal Buddha Statue made of Bronze in sitting position, one of the large beautiful Buddha images in Thailand, Phra Yok Chiang Rai; the new Emerald Buddha Statue, Phra Chedi; the ancient pagoda which registered as a national archaeological site, and a museum in the temple.

- ❑ See **The Phraya Mung Rai Memorial** in Chiang Rai Town. Phraya Mung Rai was 25th king of the old kingdom (of Laos and Thailand at the present) and the 1st king of Lanna Kingdom who established Chiang Rai and Chiang Mai. There are many places named after his name in both provinces.

Figure 258 The clock tower in Chiangrai

❑ Discover a beautiful and spectacular design of **The Clock Tower in the center of Chiang Rai** and see lights and sound played from the clock tower at 8 pm.

❏ Ride a speed boat along **Kok River**; the main river of Chiang Rai which originated from Myanmar, flows to Thailand at Mae Eye District in Chiang Mai, Chiang Rai through Mae Khong River at Chiang Saen District.

Figure 259 Wat Rong khun, The White Temple

❏ Visit **Wat Rong Khun**; a beautiful temple which is known as "The White Temple" among tourists. The main ordination hall is built in Lanna Art style in white color. The temple was built in 1997, designed by Ajarn Chalermchai Kositpipat; the wellknown artist in Thailand, who wished to build a temple architectures like a heavenly city that can be touched by humans.

❑ See **Mae Sai Boundary Post;** the checkpoint to Myanmar located **in Mae Sai District**; 63 kilometers from downtown. Talad Mae Sai or Mae Sai Market has been one of the remarkable places where tourists never missed coming here for shopping and get photo at the border. It's the mostnorth district of Thailand; it's where you can cross the border to Tha Khi Lek province in Myanmar.

❑ Travel to Mae sai can be done from Bangkok by public buses directly to this district. You can check schedule from Morchit Northern Bus Terminal and some of other tour-buses from private companies. Buses are also available from other provinces directly here.

❑ Attractions in Maesai district such as; Wat Phrathat Doi Tung, Pla Cave, Wat Phrathart Doi Wow, Doi Nang Non and Waldpark Tham Luang-Khun Nam Nang Non.

Figure 260 Mae Sai

❏ Visit Wat Tham Pla or Fish Cave in Mae Sai; an old temple where a small stream and fish flowing under the limestone cave of the mountain. There are lots of monkeys around here.

Figure 261 Wat Tham Pla

❏ Ride a local pick-up or "Song Thaew" **for Doi Tung;** a mountain of Daen Lao Mountain Range where there are many places for admiring.

Figure 262 PhraTamnak Doi Tung

❖ Admire **Phra Thamnak Doi Tung**; a palace located
at Mae Fah Luang District on the ridge of Nang Non
Mountain, about 1,200 meters high. This palace was
established in simple designs and decorations built in
1987 for Her Majesty Somdej Phra Sri Nakarinthara
Borom Rathcha-chon-nanee; King Bhumibol's mother,
who initiated in forest preservation in Doi Tung areas,
planted many trees and made a beautiful landscape
surroundings with gardens of winter flowers and also
helped those Hill Tribe Villagers to have a better
quality of lives from their local products here for
selling to the public and tourists.

Figure 263 Wat Phrathat Doi Tung

❖ Admire **Phra Thart Doi Tung**; the sacred pagoda contained of Buddha's Relic from long time ago. There is the annual festival for worshipping tradition for Buddha which is by walking to the pagoda with flowers on the hill.

❖ Admire Mae Fah Luang Garden; a fabulous garden of winter flowers blooming in front of Phra Thamnak Doi Tung. (November- February)

❖ Adventurous for **Doi Tung Tree Top Walk** and zip – line jumps.

❖ Visit the **Hall of Inspiration**; the halls exhibit the Thai royal family history and a museum from their inspirations and all works for people in the country. Their determinations are for improving quality of life. It's worth for visiting.

❖ Shop a souvenir from local hill tribe villagers. The products are handmade from Doi Tung.

❑ Watch a beautiful sunrise at **Phu Chee Dao**; a hill with its peak point to the sky, the height is about 1,800 meters above sea level. See a nice view of Mae Khong River and forest surroundings.

Figure 264 Phu Chee Dao, Chiangrai

❏ **Tham Luang-Khun Nam Nang Non National Park;** the best known in the world about 12 boys and a trainer got lost in the cave about 15 days. The mountain is about 8 kms from town, the tourists are allowed to see inside the cave. Must visit.

Figure 265 Tham Luang Khun Nam Nang Non

❑ Climb to the top of **Phu Chee Fah**; a popular hilltop for all tourists, away from town about 90 kilometers, located in Thoeng District. When I first time came here, it's not so convenient like nowadays but we enjoyed hiking to the top of this hill at 4 am to admire a beautiful sunrise and back to sleep in a small tent and drank fresh air here.

Figure 266 Phu Chee Fah

❑ Hike to **Doi Pha Tang**; one of a picturesque sunrise and sunset on the hill destination for trekkers and also can see Mae Khong River and Phu Chee Fa Hill at the hill top. It's in Wiang Kaen District; 25 kilometers from Phu Chee Fah.

Figure 267 Doi Pha Tang

❑ Visit **Chiang Khong District**; a place where you can cross the Mae Khong River to Laos at Ban Hua Wiang; a popular place for tourist's accommodation. You can also ride a boat to Luang Phra Bang in Laos. The buses are available for Chiang Khong at The Bus Terminal in Chiang Rai Town.

❑ Visit **Wat Champa** in Chiang Khong.The temple is located near Khong River. It's abandoned for a long time, but it's announced as a temple in 2012. The architecture was built in Lanna Style.

❑ Admire **The Giant Buddha** Statue on the hilltop of **Wat Thep Nimit, the boundary of Siam.**

❑ See the fresh water big fish aquarium.

❑ **Ride a bus to Chiang Khong Boundary Post in Chiang Khong for travelling to Luang Phra Bang in Laos.** The bus rides to Huaixai by crossing Mae Khong River, then ride a slow boat to Luang Phra Bang. It takes about 30 hours there; by staying overnight along the way.

The trip to Laos by boat is slow because of the river tides, rapids and rocks on the river all the river route but you can enjoy naturally beautiful scenery and   local lives along river bank during the trip.

❑ Visit **Chiang Saen**; an ancient city of The Lanna Kingdom,   where The Mae Khong River borders the north end of the district and become the boundary with Laos. It's about 15 kilometers from Chiang Khong District. The ancient Chiang Saen City was found in 1325 by Phra Chao Saen Phu, the Ruler of Lanna Kingdom. There are many ruins found in town at the archaeological site in town:

❑ Admire the old pagoda at **Wat Pa Sak**; its name came from 300 teak planted around the areas found at the archaeological site in Chiang Saen Town. You should see the old **city wall** of Chiang Saen Town.

❑ Discover **The Golden Triangle at Chiang Saen**; the area where the borders of Thailand, Laos and Myanmar meet with each other.

❑ Discover beautiful scenery of The Golden Triangle from **Wat Phra Thart Pha Gnow.**

❑ Shop at Chiang Saen Pier.

❑ Explore Mae Khong River; the 10th longest river in the world with the length about 4800 kilometers, at Chiang Saen Pier; the pier of mainly business transaction among the four countries; Thailand, China, Laos and Myanmar. You can catch a big boat to **Xishuangbanna Autonomous Prefecture** at Kuan Loei Pier in China. The trip along Mae Khong River from Chiang Saen to China; is slow because of rapids, takes about 12 hours for 265 kilometers there; admire the riversides scenery and visit a small village there.

❑ Stroll around a hill tribe village **at Doi Pha Hee**; a great place for mountains view and homestay.

Figure 268 Pha Hee Village

❑ Have a coffee at **Doi Pha Mei; a** Hill of hill tribe residential areas; nearby Pha Hei, and walk along a narrow lanes to a valley to view the Pha Mei Hill.

❑ Drink a cup of a good quality tea at **Rai Cha Choui Fong**.

❑ Taste a local famous dessert "Bua **Loy**"; a flour mixed with taro boiled in coconut milk or ice cream, at the walking street in town.

❑ **Eat local food** of Northern Region; Khao Soi, Noodles and ribs soup, Nam Prik Noom, Sai Oui or local homemade-sausage, Clab Moo; a crispy pork skin etc.

❑ See the **Parade of the Hill tribe people** in Chiang Rai during December-January; the annual cherry-blossom festival of their culture shows and products.

❑ Enjoy **The Singha Park**; a scenic park setting for relaxation. It's a place where the Village Of Illumination Festival performed in winter.

DOI
MAE
SALONG

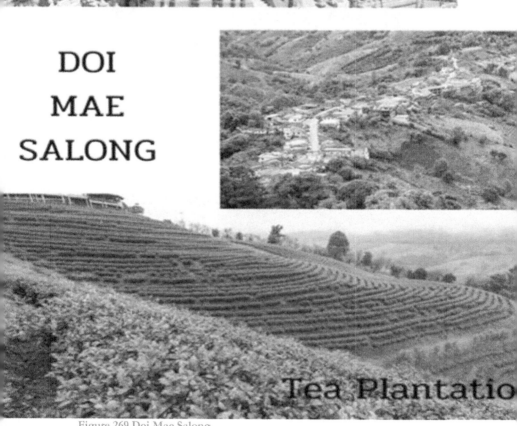

Tea Plantatio

Figure 269 Doi Mae Salong

❑ If you arrive Chiangrai before Chiang Mai, you can stop by **Doi Mae Salong** before going to Chiang Mai Province; it's by passing through Mae Chan District about 65 kilometers to the hill. It's a hill where the Chinese Refugees; Kuomintang Military Army, known as Chinese Nationalist Party, were expelled from Burma and settled near Doi Mae Salong since about 1961. The place was on the ridge of Mae Salong Hill and was called Mae Salong Village; its name changed to Santikhiri Village when all Chinese become Thai Citizen in 1978.

❑ Backpack to stay at **Doi Mae Salong** Hill. You can ride a minibus in Chiang Rai for here.

❑ Drink hot **Oolong-tea**; a high grade traditional Chinese Tea at **Santikhiri Town**; It's the fertile land for growing high mountain Oolong tea; the main production of tea from Chiang Rai and famous among visitors.

❑ Discover a beautiful large Chinese style Shrine Building which is **The Martyrs' Memorial** for the Chinese soldiers who helped the Thai Army fought with Communist Party in Thailand. There are many information displayed for the history of this town.

❑ Admire **Phra Thart Si Maha Phot Mongkon Bunchum;** a temple-center of Mae Salong People. See the Myanmar frontier from the top here.

❑ See **The General Tuan Shi-Wen Tomb;** which is on the hilltop where you can visit and enjoy a nice panoramic view of the Santikhiri town.

Figure 270 Santikhiri at doi Mae salong

THANK YOU
KOB KHUN KA

ABOUT AUTHOR

Name: Varani Bumrungluck
Born: 4th Jan, 1958 in Thailand
A.B. English from Far Eastern University
Tourist Guide License No. 11-76006
Award: Best Sales Manager Award of Toyota's Dealer received from Toyota Motor (Thailand) Co., Ltd. in 2006.
My email address: varaniluck@gmail.com
varaniweb@gmail.com

Working Experiences:

I started my job as a tourist guide at a travel agent in Bangkok in 1985 until "Black May", a crackdown on protesters in 1992, resulting in an impact on the tour business.

I changed my job to work at a private company as a secretary to the owner for six years. I found that working in an office was not my type so I moved to Chiang Mai for trying a coffee shop and restaurant business. I lived in Chiang Mai for few years but I did not succeed; according to the location which was not suitable and our investment money was not enough then I came back to Bangkok and finally got a new job at the Toyota car-dealer in Samut Sakon province as a salesman. It took 12 years working at the car-dealers; two were Toyota and the other was Mazda as a salesman, sales manager and general manager until I retired at 58 years old.

I thought that life nearly 60s was not only relaxation and waiting for death, so I decided to join my old friends who still worked at a travel agent I used to be a tourist guide in the past. I was very glad when I still was welcomed warmly.

But this time I became a sales representative at the tour counter. In fact, I liked to be a tourist guide but the office recommended me to work at the tour counter instead. I found that selling car challenged my skill by monitoring the numbers of sales to achieve all the targets set for monthly, quarterly and yearly which I had to plan ahead, followed up my prospects but always succeeded every target, but the tour sales were very tough; closing sales with the tourists all over the world in a limited time were more challenged because I never had a chance to follow-up. But I came back to work this job because I loved it. I always did my best to help people I met to get the most benefits for their trips in Thailand. Since there has been an outbreak of Covid-19 all over the world, all tour business and some others in Thailand have been stopped and closed, most people adapt themselves (included myself) for online business. When my account for Amazon KDP was approved, I was very glad to have job to do and found that I still had a chance to connect my guests all over the world again from my tour books, even it's the most challenged job in my life, I have still wanted to try my best to be tourist guide from the books I wrote. I would like to thank all KDP teams and my clients who support my books sincerely and I hope you enjoy Thailand trip in the near future.

Business online; Amazon KDP: Author name: Supennee K.B./Penny V.B.

http://www.facebook.com/varani.bumrungluck

Figure 271 Wat Rong Sue Ten, Chiangrai

THANK YOU, KHOB KHUN KHA

Made in the USA
Middletown, DE
26 February 2022

61861053R00263